Confessions of a Self-Help Junkie

words **Linda Pruce**
art **Kristin Smedley**
layout **Tomara Arrington**

Self Published by Circle of Women Wellness, LLC.
Circle of Women Wellness, LLC
Frederick, MD
First published in United States of America
2008

ISBN 978-0-615-25918-5

All information contained in *Confessions Of A Self-Help Junkie* is for informational, educational and entertainment purposes only. The author of this book does not dispense medical or mental health advice nor prescribe the use of any technique as a form of treatment. You are encouraged to speak with a qualified health care professional with regards to any physical, mental or emotional difficulties.

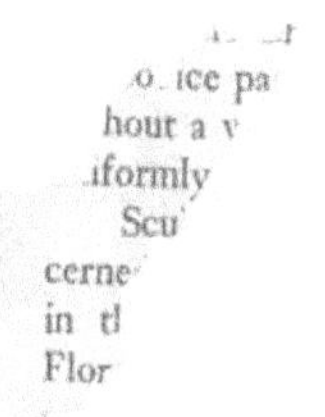

Contents

Are You A Self-Help Junkie? 1

Change Your Life TV 3

Zukav's World 5

Analysis Paralysis 6

Where Is My Soul, Anyway? 11

Self Monitor 13

Are You F.I.N.E? 14

You're Not Alone 17

How Does Your Garden Grow? 18

Are You Balanced? 20

Are You An Information Addict? 22

What Are Your Missing Pieces? 24

How to Be Courageous? 27

Self Correct 29

Confidence 30

The Simple Life 34

Seeing the Signs 37

Setting Intentions for Change 40

The Two Most Powerful Words 41

The "Right Now" Disease 43

Sunday Bloody Sunday 45

Constant Change 47

Put On Your Mask 50

Your Mission If You Choose To Accept It 53

Are You A Self-Help Junkie?

"You cannot change what you don't acknowledge." ~ *Dr. Phillip McGraw*

Life is obviously about learning, but being educated is different from being trained. Training prepares you and gives you confidence, but you become educated by experience. Reading a sex education manual teaches you about fallopian tubes, testicles, and the importance of condoms, but demanding an adequate amount of foreplay and knowing that you like to be touched, there, there, and oh, right there, takes a skill that only years of bad sex can provide.

I am of the opinion that self-help junkies are experts at training themselves in lieu of actually experiencing life and adjusting as necessary. They attend workshops and listen to experts that tell them what they should do with their lives. When that approach fails they turn to best-selling books written by different experts with competing theories and give those a shot for a while. Since the self-help genre covers a wide range of topics: health, wellness, alternative health, mental health, spirituality, religion, and the metaphysical realm, over time their honorable attempt to *improve thyself*, becomes a desperate effort to transform all aspects of their life.

Are you a self-help junkie in need of a major overhaul? Do you excel at helping others find the inner child crouching behind a brutal elementary school memory, yet if asked to help yourself, clueless as to what you need?

Often Self Help Junkies Are Poor Risk Takers

At some level you prefer controlled environments and predictable outcomes. You like the comfort of your comfort zone, even when it keeps you in a shitty space that sucks the life force right out of you. Yet you believe that there are right and wrong ways to do things in life so you spend time researching as to how you should proceed. You prefer to read about topics instead of learning by trial and error. You are not much of a risk taker, and if you do take an occasional perilous plunge, it is probably a calculated one.

Feedback Is Crucial To You

You were probably a good student that enjoyed learning, taking tests and most importantly earning high marks. You liked the recognition you received from a report card or comments written in the margins of a term paper. Feedback from your boss at work is crucial, and more than anything, you enjoy and perhaps require that the people in your life acknowledge your every contribution. Phrases like, "I like how you organized the Tupperware in the bottom cabinet," or "That lipstick color really makes your teeth look whiter," thrill you in ways that you can't quite put into words. But when it comes to applying your knowledge to new or foreign situations, you get nervous. You need to know for certain if your plans are foolproof, so you spend a great deal of time consulting with others before setting your plans in motion.

Information Keeps You In Denial

Your procrastination is disguised as research. By reading books, surfing the Internet, or gathering opinions, you give the impression that you are being proactive. In actuality, you're delaying doing much of anything. Lucky for you it will take years for people to figure this out about you and for you to admit this yourself.

It's likely that friends and family see you as conscientious and knowledgeable. In sharp contrast to the impulsive people in your life, your lack of initiative helps you avoid failing, but keeps you from launching into successful endeavors as well.

You Covet Those That Are Controversial

Those in your life that are spontaneous or uninhibited secretly excite you. Perhaps you are jealous of the black sheep in your family that flies by the seat of his or her pants. Yet you wonder how they can feel comfortable risking failure as they attempt to create changes in their life. If they do fail, you feel better knowing that you would have researched the topic prior to proceeding. But if they succeed, you are impressed by their ability to take chances and try new things without consulting others or heeding warnings.

You may need to get quiet. If you spend all of your time researching, you'll miss the answers when they come to you.

Intuition Freaks You Out

When you do, by chance, listen to a gut feeling and it works, you become confused. Admitting that you have an internal guidance system already in place, although exciting, scares you because it goes against everything you know to be true and logical in the world. You want to believe that you have good instincts, but you are scared to break away from your need to have a guarantee before proceeding.

It's Time To Graduate

Unlike your school years when finals determined that studying could cease or graduation meant that you had earned enough credits for a diploma, real life involves learning on a daily basis. Most people find their strength by being thrust into a new situation and succeeding without having all of the answers. You have done this millions of times but may not recognize your skill at being adaptable and flexible. Therefore you may need to get quiet. If you spend all of your time researching, you'll miss the answers when they come to you. This is especially true when answers arrive disguised as a child's honest remark, lyrics to a favorite song, or a random conversation with a homeless man on the subway.

Research Intuition

If your addiction to self-help information persists, then consider spending your free time researching intuition instead. Pick up *Awakening Intuition*, by Dr. Mona Lisa Shultz and check out her web site: www.drmonalisa.com. Click on "radio shows" and listen to Segment Two on how to balance your intellect with intuition. Not only will it improve your skills, it may help to get that monkey off your back once and for all.

- How many self-help books do you own?
- How many self-help magazines and Web sites do you browse?
- Are you constantly looking outside yourself for answers?
- Are you tired and frustrated?

I have spent a large portion of the last decade reading self-help books. I would decide that there was something terribly wrong with me, purchase a book that would light the way to change, vow to change, change for a little while, revert back to my old behaviors, and oh yeah, feel like a big loser. I always started out strong only to fizzle out in the end before meeting goals, sometimes even before setting goals. Frankly, it's all Oprah's fault and I blame her entirely.

Change Your Life TV

I officially became a self-help junkie in September of 1998. I was sitting on my bed, minding my own business, breastfeeding my newborn and wondering whether it would be wrong to smoke a cigarette while nursing. As I was figuring out the logistics of this dilemma – *Could I reach my cigarettes without breaking the baby's seal on my breast? Could I blow the smoke towards the window instead of up the nostrils of my daughter? And, how do you explain a burn mark on the cheek of a 6-week-old?* – as I caught the start of Oprah's fall season.

Change Your Life TV was the new theme. "I want to use television as the medium for communicating to people a way to better their lives," Oprah told TV Guide that year. Apparently informing folks while entertaining them wasn't good enough, transforming them was the new mission of the program.

Good God, she was speaking to me! I was a fat, tired, chain-smoking mother of two with a traveling "I'm-only-home-on-the-weekends" husband. I definitely needed a change. Rather than reaching for my smokes, I grabbed my bedside journal and feverishly began taking notes.

It seemed simple enough. All I had to do was tune in every afternoon and slowly craft the life of my dreams. I would lose weight, stop smoking, find my passion, improve my marriage, and raise my kids in a calm and loving manner, all while honoring my authentic self.

It was perfect. Experts and published authors would tell me exactly what I needed to do to change my life. Oprah, the poster-child for life improvement, would moderate the proceedings. How could I lose? Success was virtually guaranteed, so I tuned in daily and began the exhilarating process of creating a life of authentic power.

Now this is the part of the story where I am supposed to insert the depressing details of my horrific existence. The sad-but-true tails of a life spun completely out of control. Yet there's nothing major to report to you. No nasty parental divorce stories, alcoholic escapades, abusive husband tales, infertility woes, progressive diseases, sexual harassment lawsuits or bankruptcy tidbits to tell you about. I really and truly had nothing to complain about.

Sure, my husband worked out-of-state four days a week, leaving me home alone to care for two young children. Yes, it was stressful at times. Certainly I was feeling lost transitioning from a having a career to having children to raise full time. But the bills got paid, I had a beautiful home, the fridge was filled, I was married to a man who loved me, had lots of supportive friends along with a healthy relationship with my family and no one in my life had been diagnosed with a terminal illness. I had the life most people wanted.

My life wasn't the problem. I was the problem. My right, creative brain was longing for something more that I couldn't quite identify while my left, analytical brain was certain that I had too much to be unsatisfied. Intuitively I knew that my life was supposed to be different, but for the life of me, I was clueless as to what it was supposed to look like.

When Oprah's first expert, John Gray, took the stage and became the first official "Change Your Life" guru, I tuned in determined to craft the life of my desire. What I never imagined was the Pandora's Box that I was about to peer into.

Soon I was blaming my mother . . .

According to Dr. Gray there were twelve blocks to personal success that needed to be removed from my life for contentment to be obtained. I merely needed to link each block to a specific feeling to break free from my pathetic life. I learned that my indifference directly corresponded to feelings of powerlessness. Why? Well, because John Gray with the PH.D. told me that it did. This powerlessness stemmed from my past, which also created feelings of sorrow, frustration, disappointment and worry. I was instructed to explore these emotions by linking each feeling to a previous situation; writing feeling letters to those that had created any chaos in my life; releasing all negativity and forgiving anyone I had unfinished business with. Once I did all of that, I could move on to the next block that was getting in my way.

Eventually, I churned up so many different emotions that I wasn't sure what my blocks were and what feelings I needed to delve into. Luckily, Dr. Gray tapped into his ready-made audience and penned a book that would give specifics on how to create personal success.

Convinced that I was a mere 300 pages away from enlightenment, I bought his book *How To Get What You Want And Want What You Have*. Soon I was blaming my mother, writing feeling letters to dead relatives and hating my husband. Instead of wanting what I had, I was ashamed of what I had created. Rather than changing my reality I began berating my history. By the time I closed the back cover, I was still fat, smoking, and unhappy, but at least I despised everyone else in my life as much as myself.

Oprah's guests, on the other hand, were all making great strides. Each day someone would have the ever so popular, yet allusive "A-Ha Moment" right on national television. Why wasn't I getting the same Oprah show results at home?

I decided that I needed some spiritual Ex-lax to unconstipate my emotional self so I surfed the Web, took on-line personality tests and read a different self-help book each week. Like a student preparing for finals, I was determined to earn an "A" in personal development.

My children didn't get it, wanting instead to be fed and nurtured, but I needed to break through my blocks so that I could be a better mom! I'd pop in a video, sit next to my daughter and write more letters. While breastfeeding my baby I would stew in anger, blaming my own mother for not breastfeeding me. Because my husband was too busy working, traveling and providing food and shelter to assist me in my self-help journey, I hired a cleaning lady to come weekly so that I would have time to read and focus on my issues. I bought frozen dinners to serve to my toddler and began living on a diet of coffee and cigarettes. I was on a mission, damn it! Nutritious foods would have to wait! And since it would be wrong to blow tobacco toxins around my kids, I excused myself regularly from my family and hid upstairs in my office where I could surf online self-help sites and smoke my brains out.

Why wasn't I getting the same Oprah show results at home?

I figured that cable television's Nick Jr. could teach my toddler, Paige, how to read. I was busy and besides, they did it in Technicolor with cartoon characters and upbeat background music. I further deduced that Paige should learn early how to be self-sufficient, so I lined the bottom shelf of the refrigerator with juice cups and placed individual containers filled with snacks within her reach.

"Mom, the baby's crying!" Paige would yell.
"Just turn the crank on the swing and she'll go back to sleep," I'd yell back.
"I'm hungry."
"Grab some Cheez-Its," I'd reply.
"I think the baby pooped in her diaper."
"Paige, I'm busy up here. She just farted, that's all. Watch Mr. Rogers."
"He's boring."
"He's a genius. He taught me everything when I was your age."
"I don't like him."
"Grab the remote and hit 3-1. Blues Clues is on!"

As I went deeper into my psyche, my constipation only worsened. Like the old Pepto Bismo commercials where people would explode from an abdominal wave of in-di-gest-ion, I was suffering from in-dig-na-tion, agg-ra-va-tion and frus-tra-tion.

I was a personal mess instead of a success, but now I was painfully aware of my complete and total failure. I lit up a cigarette, took a long, hard drag and told myself I would have to face the facts. *Maybe I'm just a fuck-up. Perhaps I'm destined to just be an average mom and wife with addictive tendencies and thunder thighs. Perhaps personal passion is overrated. Maybe this is the life of my dreams.*

But then I heard a familiar voice in the background. Oprah was singing her theme song. It was 4:00 eastern standard time and my self-help sister was coming on air.

"Gary Zukav says your life is a journey to learn about yourself. From the time we're born, we're enrolled in what he calls the Earth School. There are no tests, no grades, and nobody flunks," she instructed.

Nobody flunks? This is right up my alley, I thought to myself. I'm not a screw-up. I'm just a student in the Earth School trying to graduate. I bet this Zukav guy knows just what I need.

I grabbed my journal and yelled down to Paige.
"There's a sippy cup in the fridge," I said.
"Can we go outside?" she asked.
"In a minute," I said.
"How long is a minute?" she asked.
"When Oprah is over," I lied.

The Seat Of The Soul. I'd better write that down. We can go to the bookstore after Oprah, and I'll take the kids to *McDonalds* for dinner. The baby can sleep in the carrier while Paige plays in the ball pit and I read. This is the answer. I can feel it!

Nobody flunks? This is right up my alley, I thought to myself. I'm not a screw-up.

Zukav's World

When I first saw Gary Zukav on *Oprah*, I thought he was rather strange. Normally I'd write off the advice of anyone that I felt was weird or bizarre, but since Oprah liked him I figured I'd give him a chance. That's a big problem with self-help junkies: we worship the Oprah Goddess and will do whatever she says. Thankfully she has never asked a Satanist to fly to Chicago on American Airlines (the official airline of *The Oprah Winfrey Show*) and reveal his teachings to the world.

But my Oprah-knows-all theory was grounded in logic. She has gone from an outhouse in the segregated south to a penthouse in downtown Chicago. She's successful in a career that just so happens to correspond to her passion in life. She's been real enough with her audience to share her failures as well as her triumphs. And she has enough fact checkers, researchers and a large enough production budget to ensure that her experts aren't complete and total quacks. Plus, I was desperate, so I bought Zukav's book

The Seat Of The Soul is Gary Zukav's take on evolution. In it he claims that we are a five sensory specious evolving into a multi-sensory species. In other words, we as human beings have six, not five, senses. If we utilized this sixth, intuitive sense it would become a faculty as reliable as our other five.

Would we all just start seeing dead people? Not exactly. Zukav postulates that the fittest that survive aren't

The problem was that the logical left hemisphere of my brain would not be downsized. It had functioned as the CEO of my life for thirty years and was not going to be brushed aside without a fight.

necessarily those with the most physical dominance and power. Rather, the "fittest" among us would be the people who chose to use their physical dominance and power in the most reverent and honorable of ways. People so tuned in to the bigger, spiritual picture that using their power to victimize or harm others would not be a part of their consciousness.

The Seat Of The Soul was the first book I read to acknowledged that my sixth, intuitive sense, had the same amount of credence as that which I could prove via sight, smell, taste, hearing and touch. This information, although freeing, was frightening on some level. I had spent my entire life attempting to logically and systematically create a life for myself. Believing that perceptions and gut feelings were more important than following a practical plan in life, transformed my self-help journey from one of discovery to desperation. What the hell were my perceptions and more importantly, how could I tap into my intuition on a regular basis?

Rather than calming down, getting quiet and trusting my inner voice, I became obsessed with trying to figure out how to get this voice to speak to me loud and clear, and as often as possible. Should I commune with angels or balance my chakras? Would the tarot give me insight or did I need to give Dionne Warrick a call? Maybe if I sat in the lotus position during yoga I could "Om" my way to authenticity. Perhaps the Goddess could turn up the volume on the intuitive, feminine aspect of my psyche, or maybe Jesus alone would give me the answers I was searching for?

The problem was that the logical left hemisphere of my brain would not be downsized. It had functioned as the CEO of my life for thirty years and was not going to be brushed aside without a fight. Logical me needed information so it stimulated the motor strip of my cerebral cortex and forced me to shower, shave my legs, gloss my lips and show up weekly at my local Borders Books and Music store to browse the self-help, inspirational and metaphysical shelves. Because the brain's nutrient of choice is glucose, it also led me to the in-store café to regularly fuel up on grande, no-whip mochaccinos and cinnamon scones.

Analysis Paralysis

I justified spending all of my free time at Borders as my mommy escape. It was the place where I could forget about my full-time mothering duties and lose myself in books and information. I could pretend that I was stocking up for a non-existent book club and because my husband was never home and didn't pay the bills, he was clueless as to what I was spending there. I see now that my need for spiritual speed was a way for me to avoid and tune out of the life I was living.

If I really wanted to shame myself, I would quote to you excerpts from my personal journals. Pathetic entries filled with 1-part doubt, 10-parts self-hatred, 2 cups of broken promises, and seasoned to taste with a variety of *should-of's, could-of's, would-of's*, and *I'm definitely going to's*.

Rather than shutting up long enough to allow my authentic self to emerge, I filled my head with expert opinions, self-help exercises, and new age theories. Of course a true self-help junkie knows that "it's all good." Since everything happens for a reason, and when you know better you'll do better, regrets are only for the spiritually underdeveloped. Any new-ager will tell you that I would not be where I am today if I hadn't spent so much time reading, thinking, writing, expressing, rethinking, and attempting to create positive and lasting change in my life. But for every self-help junkie out there justifying wasted time, there's a doer that's learning by trial and error and getting further along.

The ugly truth hit me square in my third eye when I was moving furniture around in my home. I decided to transfer all of my books from one bookcase to another. As I glanced at each title I made a shocking discovery. I had close to fifty self-help books in my possession. As I began to process the fact that I had unconsciously turned my den into a New Age bookstore, I decided to further my depression by turning over each book and adding up what I've spent on this compendium of insight and knowledge. An hour into this process I was forced to stop and ask myself an important question. *How could I read so many books and still not be a highly-empowered-self-help-master-of-the-universe?*

My failure would be easier to accept if I wasn't smart. But I took AP calculus in high school for Christ's sake and went on to earn a Master's degree. I knew that I was intelligent. Why didn't I have more to show for it?

Because of this I will, without shame, share with you the contents and retail value of my bookcase in no particular order. Mind you, only the strongest books survived the three subsequent moves since the start of my self-help journey. If I had kept a complete and accurate tally of books, magazines, subliminal tapes, and Internet printouts, I'm sure I'd have two bookcases to report on.

Anatomy Of The Spirit *by Caroline Myss: $14.00*
Chakras are cool. Learning about them via a religious paradigm was especially helpful. But when you're introduced to an unfamiliar, mystical methodology, it's easy to want to scrap your belief system and embrace something new.
Mistake #1: Deciding that I had to learn a completely new system instead of integrating this information into the belief system that I had at that time.
Mistake #2: Becoming obsessed with researching chakras instead of recognizing that this clearly indicated an imbalance in my third chakra center.

Dr. Myss' book as insightful and inspiring as it was, became an obsession in which I allowed her recommendations to morph from "how tos" to "must dos" which sent me way off course for years rather than taking what I needed and leaving the rest behind.

Why People Don't Heal And How They Can *by Caroline Myss: $22.50*
I got the why people don't heal part – it's the how they can aspect that I'm still working on. I have this bizarre notion that when I'm diagnosed with something terminal, this book will be helpful, so I rarely allow anyone to borrow it, just in case.

How To Get What You Want And Want What You Have *by John Gray: $24.95*
Honestly, he had me hook, line and sinker until the vitamin love section. That was bizarre. But I loved the notion of releasing negative energy before calling positive energy into the body. Good little tip from Uncle John that I use when I remember.

Women's Bodies, Women's Wisdom *by Dr. Christiane Northrup: $17.95*
An excellent reference book that is a must have for anyone that menstruates. My favorite part is when she states, "For me, having young children was – bar none – the most taxing part of my life, a time that I wouldn't care to repeat again unless I had two beloved nannies, sisters, or friends living with me full time to help with child care."

Finally, I gave myself permission to not enjoy every aspect of motherhood and to accept that hosting tea parties with imaginary animals and a 3-year-old wasn't my forte and that was okay. Her *book*

I have this bizarre notion that when I'm diagnosed with something terminal, this book will be helpful, so I rarely allow anyone to borrow it, just in case.

suggested to me that perhaps I'd enjoy motherhood more when my daughters were older and I did not, in fact, have to love and adore every stage of their development to consider myself to be a "good mom".

The Wisdom Of Menopause *by Dr. Christiane Northrup: $18.95*
I know what you're thinking. I'm only in thirties, why the hell would I be reading about menopause? Because I'm co-dependent (see below), I wanted to help the women in my life that were going through menopause and be prepared for the future, of course.

Beyond Codependency *by Melody Beattie: $13.95*
This book allowed me to recognize that I was co-dependent. Sadly, I didn't quite get beyond it, but realizing that it was a goal to achieve was a start at least.

Seat Of The Soul *by Gary Zukav: $9.60*
I've said enough already about this book. But as you can deduce by the next entry, I was so fascinated by the seemingly thousands of readers whose life miraculously changed after reading this book, I bought his next one with the hope that it would help me find serenity.

Soul Stories *by Gary Zukav: $24.00*
I really wanted to have my own soul story. Unfortunately I was left with just another inspirational book to make my bookshelf look pretty.

Who Moved My Cheese? *by Dr. Spencer Johnson: $19.95*
This book would have been better if it had been called, Who Cut The Cheese? He then could have followed it up with, Who Licked The Knife? But I think my kids will really dig this book, so I'm glad that I own it.

Opening To Spirit *by Caroline Shola Arewa: $19.95*
Yet another homage to my Chakra system obsession, but an excellent read with an African spiritual twist that I had not stumbled on before.

One Day My Soul Just Opened Up *by Iyanla Vanzant: $13.00*
One day my wallet just opened up and I brought this book home with me. I did enjoy the information, it was the daily dedication needed to perform the exercises that I had issues with.

Spiritual Alchemy *by Dr. Christine Page: $24.95*
Obviously I'm a sucker for medical doctors that write about spiritually uplifting topics.

Something More: Excavating Your Authentic Self *by Sarah Ban Breathnach: $18.00*
When I think about this book, I think about the story of Alison, a first grader that died and her mother, Beth, who decided to hold her wake in their home. I'm sure there were other stories that touched me, but this story stuck with me. It settled into the recesses of my brain and mingles with my random thoughts. Although I require copious notes and a meticulously kept calendar to do my repeatable, daily activities, Alison stays with me, wherever I go.

The Five Tibetans *by Christopher S. Kilham: $9.95*
This book claims that five simple exercises can change your life. Can you believe that I never even tried them – ever? Five exercises for twenty minutes, daily and I couldn't do it. What the hell is wrong with me? I found out when I read…

The Dark Side Of The Light Chasers *by Debbie Ford: $11.70*
Unlike other self-helpers that only want to talk about all that is positive, Ms. Ford focused on the dangerously dark flip side of people that emerges far too often. I was officially given permission not only to expose but also acknowledge my shadow. I am forever grateful.

At The Root Of This Longing *by Carol Lee Flinders: $13.95*
An amazing book that focuses on the points at which spirituality and feminism seem to collide – vowing silence vs. finding voice, relinquishing ego vs. establishing 'self', resisting desire vs. reclaiming the body, and enclosure vs. freedom – and how they can be reconciled. To have my own feelings of longing put into words and validated was a wonderful gift to be given that I continue to treasure.

Life Strategies *by Dr. Phil McGraw: $12.95*
I never read this one. The exercises intimidated me because they represented work that was required. Back then I was more interested in finding someone to tell me what was wrong with me. Besides, once he got his own television show, watching daily became easier than reading, writing and thinking.

The Seven Spiritual Laws For Parents *by Deepak Chopra: $16.95*
Never read it. Don't tell my kids.

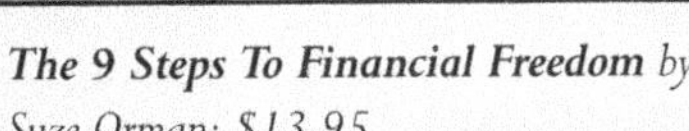

The 9 Steps To Financial Freedom *by Suze Orman: $13.95*
After browsing the beginning sections I realized that I'm already financially free because my attitude toward money is healthy. In fact, if my attitude toward the rest of my life matched my money attitude, I would have saved hundreds of dollars by not buying all of these books and be even closer to financial freedom and prosperity.

The Alchemist *by Paulo Coelho: $13.00*
I really enjoyed this book. We all want to believe that the universe is conspiring to help and not hinder us on our journey. Read this book and you will be convinced that this is so.

Spontaneous Healing
by Dr. Andrew Weil: $12.95
Here again, my quest for instant gratification got the best of me. I think it was the word spontaneous in the title that hooked me. I thought if I read the book, I would spontaneously be healed. He should have titled it, Spontaneous Healing Through Working Your Ass Off and Changing The Bullshit Way You View Your Health And Wellness.

The Change-Your-Life Quote Book
by Allen Klein: $5.99
I actually thought the book would change my life if I simply found one quote that would change my thinking. It didn't.

Don't Let Your Mind Stunt Your Growth *by Bryan E. Robinson: $10.95*
Technically I didn't buy this book. My husband received it from a conference at work. I was so impressed that my computer geek husband brought a non-technical book into the home that I stole it from him and placed it on my self-help shelf with pride.

You Can Heal Your Life
by Louise L. Hay: $17.95

You Can Heal Your Life Companion Book *by Louise L. Hay: $17.95*
I bought these books because I thought they were pretty. Seriously. They were so pretty that I didn't feel right writing in them. Sick, I know.

The Inner Child Workbook
by Cathryn L. Taylor: $16.95

Recovery Of Your Inner Child *by Lucia Capacchione: $14.00*
Both of these books fascinated me. One gave specific journal writing exercises that involve using your non-dominant hand when writing. By becoming a "lefty" when expressing myself in my journal, I was able to tap into my more intuitive right-hemisphere when communicating with myself. This simplistic idea is a journaling technique that I use often and frequently recommend to others.

The Celestine Prophecy
by James Redfield: $12.99

The Tenth Insight
by James Redfield: $13.95

The Secret Of Shambhala
by James Redfield: $14.95
Although not Pulitzer Prize winning books, they allow the reader to discover basic self-help tenets via a fictional story. This made the information interesting and easier to remember. Of course, the addict in me forced me to also buy the workbook, ***The Celestine Prophecy: An Experiential Guide*** by James Redfield and Carol Adrienne for $8.99 which I never wrote in but have just in case.

A Women's Book Of Life
by Joan Borysenko: $14.00
I loved Borysenko's other book, ***A Women's Journey To God*** that I purchased for $14.00 as well. So I automatically bought this one simply because Joan had written it. I enjoy her writing style and her outlook, but perhaps focusing on my journey to God rather than my journey through life would have sufficed.

I enjoy her writing style and her outlook, but perhaps focusing on my journey to God rather than my journey through life would have sufficed.

I do this frequently. If I like a writer I will automatically buy any follow-up creations that hit the market. I over consume only to be left with too much information to process rather than allowing the initial information to envelope and shape me over time.

Conversations With God
Series by Neale Donald Walsch

- ***Book One:*** *$24.00*
- ***Book Two:*** *$19.95*
- ***Book Three:*** *$23.00*
- ***Friendship With God:*** *$14.00*
- ***Communion With God:*** *$14.00*
- ***New Revelations:*** *$24.00*

I learned a lot from these books. Mainly that many of my own gut instincts about God, creation and the after-life are similar to what God supposedly told Mr. Walsch. Because of this, I wanted to read everything written. But I couldn't help but wonder what would have been written if a woman had a

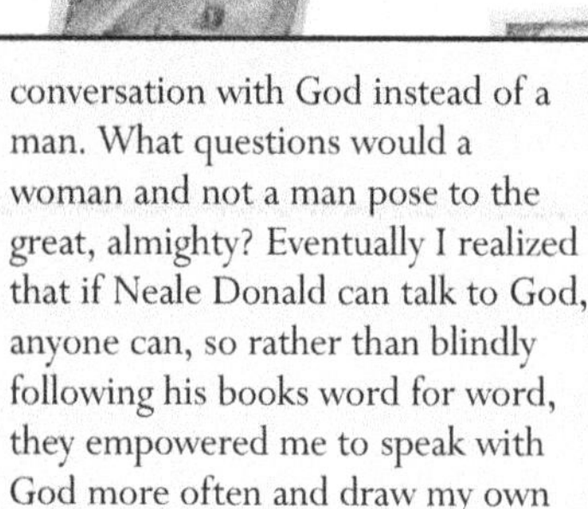

conversation with God instead of a man. What questions would a woman and not a man pose to the great, almighty? Eventually I realized that if Neale Donald can talk to God, anyone can, so rather than blindly following his books word for word, they empowered me to speak with God more often and draw my own conclusions.

A Course In Miracles: *$26.96*
Skimmed it. Interesting.

The Moon In Your Life *by Donna Cunningham: $15.95*

Moon Time *by Johanna Puangger and Thomas Poppe: $7.98*

Your Intuitive Moon *by Trish Macgregor: $14.00*
The above books fueled my research while learning about the connection between the moon and a woman's menstrual cycle. Although ***The Red Tent*** by Anita Diamant ($14.95) is a fictional tale, I include it in my self-help list. It opened me up to the moon and her many powers and lead me to other moon-themed books to learn more about the amazing satellite that circles our planet.

Learn To Power Think *by Caterina Rando: $14.95*
When I think about this book, I think about the level of my desperation. My kids and I were in Staples buying printer cartridges when I saw this in the book section. My self-help addiction was at an all time high and I almost felt like a failure if I returned home without something useful to help me on my quest. I figured that maybe my problem wasn't what I was thinking about but how I was thinking, so I brought it home convinced that I could change the way in which I used my brain. I'm sure that it is a helpful book for anyone not insane, desperate or in despair.

Circle Of Stones *by Judith Duerk: $13.95*
I love this book. Along with Dr. Northrup's ***Women's Bodies, Women's Wisdom***, if you menstruate, plan on menstruating, used to menstruate or know someone that menstruates then this book is a must read. It's simple and poetic and interesting and thought provoking. It's the gems people like me come across when were frantically searching for answers. I look forward to passing it down to my daughters with pride.

I look forward to passing it down to my daughters with pride.

Awakening Intuition *by Mona Lisa Shulz: 14.00*
In lieu of a one-on-one session with Ms. Shulz, this book is a close second. What I like the most about her writing is that she balances the intuitive information with well-documented medical information. Shulz's vast experience with brain research allows her to put her money where her mouth is. If you want to awaken your own intuition, buy this book.

Drum roll please. . .The Grand Total is: $751.51

Mind you, I haven't included tax or shipping and handling if I ordered a book online. If you add to that, Internet dial-up fees for surfing self-help sites, countless magazine purchases since 1998, and the fabulous books I bought and then gave to others, convinced that they needed to read the information as well, the total continues to climb. Of course there are also intuitive healers and mediums that I've spoken to, so that's another $500. And if my memory serves me, I think my holistic health counseling course cost me over four grand. Hmm…lets, see. If I get out my solar calculator, move closer to my window and round up, then I've spent approximately $6,000 to fail to find my authentic-soul-self.

Or did I?

Where is My Soul, Anyway?

If you've read as many self-help books as I have, then you know that the Holy Grail of self-improvement is finding the Authentic-Soul-Self. It is what all self-help junkies are searching for – the authentic, truthful, immaterial essence of who they really are. Sometimes, if you're lucky, you'll get a glimpse of your authentic-soul-self via quick flashes of insight or moments of clarity. But to be in direct and constant communication with it, you need to locate it.

Where is this self? How do you find it? Is there a secret treasure map that will lead you to the space that houses your innate intelligence and authentic intentions? Allow me to be the first to tell you that there is no DaVinci code to break, or sages that you must consult, for I know exactly where your authentic-soul-self is located.

You may have erroneously assumed that the soul is located either near the heart, which keeps you alive, or in your brain, which allows you to think and make choices. Trust me when I tell you that you are wrong.

The brain is too crowded to house the soul. It already houses the cerebellum, cranial nerves, speech and language centers and your motor strip just to name a few areas. Add in every memory, thought and all sensory and neural connections and frankly, there's already enough going on in the brain. Housing the soul there just doesn't make sense.

The heart, located smack dab in the front of your body seems too vulnerable a place to position the authentic core of your being. Because highly evolved individuals tend to lead with their heart you might think your authentic-soul-self would be located there. But with only a small, bony sternum to protect it, the heart is an easy target and open to attack and damage. Souls would be highly at risk if housed here.

If you've been looking for you're authentic-soul-self for sometime now, brace yourself, because it's behind you! In fact you're probably sitting on it, right now, which is why you've had such difficulty in locating it. Yes, you read that right. I am strongly suggesting that your soul is located in your gluteus maximus. If you think about it, it's not as absurd as it seems.

If you look carefully at the term, authentic-soul-self, and it's obvious acronym, for all intents and purposes you have been looking for your A.S.S. Now the self-help folks won't tell you this because it sounds vulgar and if you knew about this little known fact, you wouldn't buy their books. But truly, your A.S.S is what you need to find and have been desperately searching for.

If you're searching for your authentic-soul-self it is probably because you are unsure of its power and might. So it seems to reason that it would be sitting in the most controversial of body parts. Your ass is the largest muscle in your body. Yet unlike the muscles elsewhere that take great pride in being exposed, women like to hide their ass from the world with oversized clothing and tent dresses. Similarly, many women tend to hide their true self from the world so as to be accommodating and self-deprecating, since living authentically might deem you difficult, aggressive, or selfish.

The ass, otherwise known as the laurels that you rest upon when you don't feel up to the tasks of the day, would be the perfect hiding place for your true self. If

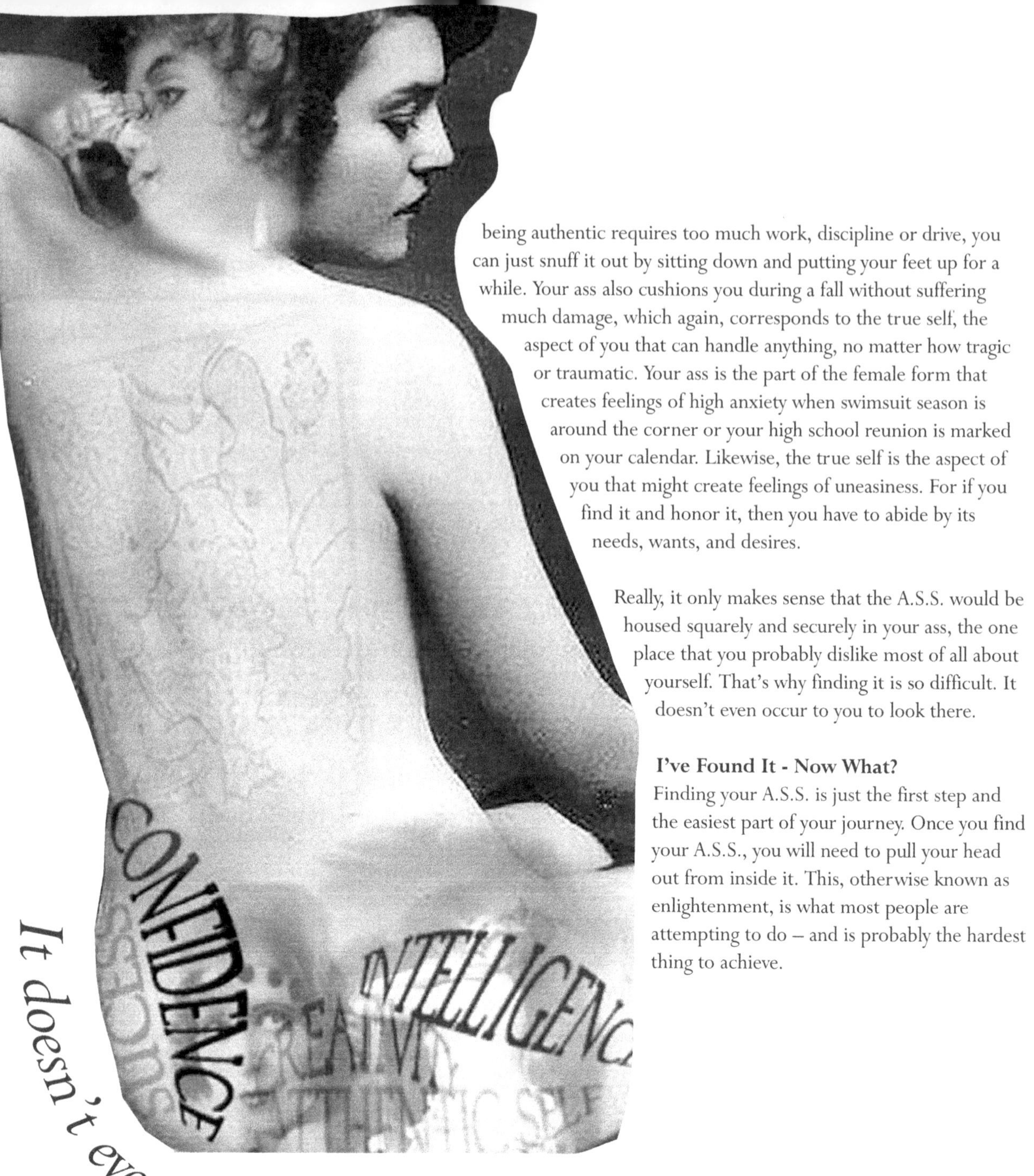

being authentic requires too much work, discipline or drive, you can just snuff it out by sitting down and putting your feet up for a while. Your ass also cushions you during a fall without suffering much damage, which again, corresponds to the true self, the aspect of you that can handle anything, no matter how tragic or traumatic. Your ass is the part of the female form that creates feelings of high anxiety when swimsuit season is around the corner or your high school reunion is marked on your calendar. Likewise, the true self is the aspect of you that might create feelings of uneasiness. For if you find it and honor it, then you have to abide by its needs, wants, and desires.

Really, it only makes sense that the A.S.S. would be housed squarely and securely in your ass, the one place that you probably dislike most of all about yourself. That's why finding it is so difficult. It doesn't even occur to you to look there.

I've Found It - Now What?

Finding your A.S.S. is just the first step and the easiest part of your journey. Once you find your A.S.S., you will need to pull your head out from inside it. This, otherwise known as enlightenment, is what most people are attempting to do – and is probably the hardest thing to achieve.

It doesn't even occur to you to look there

Self Monitor

Does my story resonate with you? Do you also spend countless hours looking outside of yourself for the answers? Do you assume that you are not smart enough to figure out what you need? Do you blindly follow the suggestions of any degreed expert or published author?

Take a breath. It's okay. There are some great self-help maestros out there that offer amazing insight into the human experience and ways in which you can reach your fullest potential. There's nothing wrong with trying to improve your life. It's only a problem if you become obsessed with leading your life in the exact manner that an expert does rather then **adapting** their suggestions to your life in a functional manner.

The following commentaries are to assist you in determining what you may need to change about your life. They are provided merely to stimulate your thinking and encourage you to become an observer when it comes to your day-to-day experience. You are not being asked to lay blame or harshly scrutinize yourself. You are simply invited to tell the truth about your experience, and note what portions of my story resonate with you.

There are exercises and confession questions sprinkled throughout this book to assist you as you delve deeper into the issues brought forth in the essays. There are no right or wrong answers. Again, you are simply asked to tell the truth.

Throughout this book tips will be offered. These are **suggestions**. Only try them if they feel right. It doesn't make me feel better about myself if you implement them. In fact I'll never know if you use them or not. I'm just telling you what worked for me. Take what you need and leave the rest behind.

Take a breath. It's okay

Are You F.I.N.E?

When I began my self-help journey, I actually believed that I was alone in my self-loathing and everyone else in my life had it all figured out. I had good friends with young children and out-of-town husbands, and knew many women unhappy in their careers and exploring a potential plan B for their lives. No one else was complaining, so I assumed that I was the one with the problem, not them.

I'm Fine!

In fact, when asked, they were all simply FINE! How's work? Fine. How are your kids? Fine. How's your husband? Fine. How are you? Fine.

What I didn't know then and only discovered years later was that fine is sometimes an acronym that stands for fucked up, insecure, neurotic, and emotional. When someone states that they are fine, chances are they are a mess. Chances are also good that they erroneously believe that you're the one with the perfect life that has it all figured out which is why they lie and tell you that they are fine in the first place.

I started to develop this theory through my newsletter. For three years I wrote a monthly women's empowerment publication. Initially when I focused on only health and wellness, I didn't get much feedback from my readers. However, when I started telling the truth about my own personal issues and sharing the highs and lows of my life each month, people would email me and, - as shocking as it sounds, - relate! When I started to tell the truth to my "fine", women friends, a funny thing happened. I found out that they weren't all that fine, either. They were confused, sad, angry, or apathetic and unsure as to how to deal with so many different emotions.

Life Cycles

When I was in my twenties, my friends and I readily admitted that we didn't know how to get what we wanted. But as we all got older, and got what we had wished for, I noticed that the personaes we showed to the world didn't match the comments and concerns that we privately shared with one another. Although grateful to have so many choices, we were overwhelmed by conflicting priorities.

My close friends are in their thirties and forties which I've discovered is an even more intense time of self-reflection. Thirty was the milestone where I and most of my friends began to closely examine our lives. We looked back on our twenties, cringed a bit and then made more mature choices based on having better information. We began to form a clearer picture as to what we truly needed and how to get it for ourselves.

Whereas my friends in their forties seem to be creating permanent changes based on what they uncovered by trial and error in their thirties. They learn from mistakes with less shame and seem ready to implement strategies with a level of confidence and clarity.

The Good News

My mother claims that at fifty, you're not as concerned about the opinions of others and that you get serious about tying up your loose ends. Gail Sheehy, author of the popular *Passages* series of books, claims that a person has a second adulthood between the ages of 45-75. This period of life involves a transitioning from survival to mastery when a person hits their "meaning crisis". This meaning crisis is somewhat spiritual in nature and based upon a person's need to: integrate the disparate aspects of themselves, their hunger for wholeness, their need to know the truth. It is a time when women and men pursue their passions and fill their need to interact significantly with the world and extend experiences beyond themselves.

In other words, as you age, the learning, experimenting and risk taking never stops. God only knows what happens at seventy-five. I think you begin to cuss more, go bra-less on a regular basis, and not care at all about what anyone thinks of you.

Be Fine With Being F.I.N.E.

If Sheehy and the many wise women in my life are correct, then it's best to relax and enjoy the ride. The key, I'm guessing is to be fine with being F.I.N.E. And if you can tell the truth about this to the people that you care about, you can stay sane in the process.

Talking, it turns out, can be the key to finding workable solutions. Dr. Mona Lisa Shulz, author of *Awakening Intuition*, states that intuitive insight uses the right side of the brain whereas verbal expression uses the logical, left side of the brain. Thus by saying out loud what you think and feel you use both your intellect and intuition for problem solving.

By saying out loud what you only think privately, you steal the thunder from your negative, inner voice and it will stop contradicting you because frankly you've sucked the fun from it. This is no different then when the kid with new glasses calls herself four-eyes before anyone else can. If she's the first to state the obvious, no one else will yell out a comment and embarrass her.

By speaking your truth to others and silencing your inner critic, you will allow yourself a moments peace to determine the steps that you need to take and setting them into motion on your own timetable. By telling others when you are **f**ucked up, **i**nsecure, **n**eurotic and **e**motional, you can be **f**ree from the **i**nsidious, **n**egative **e**xchange that you constantly have with yourself. Then you can actually be fine as in "okay" and mean it.

Remember that you are not alone in your confusion. Take a chance and have faith that the people in your life will be able to relate, and accept you with all your faults. By having honest conversations will the people in your world, the answers will materialize faster and you can enjoy the process instead of running from it.

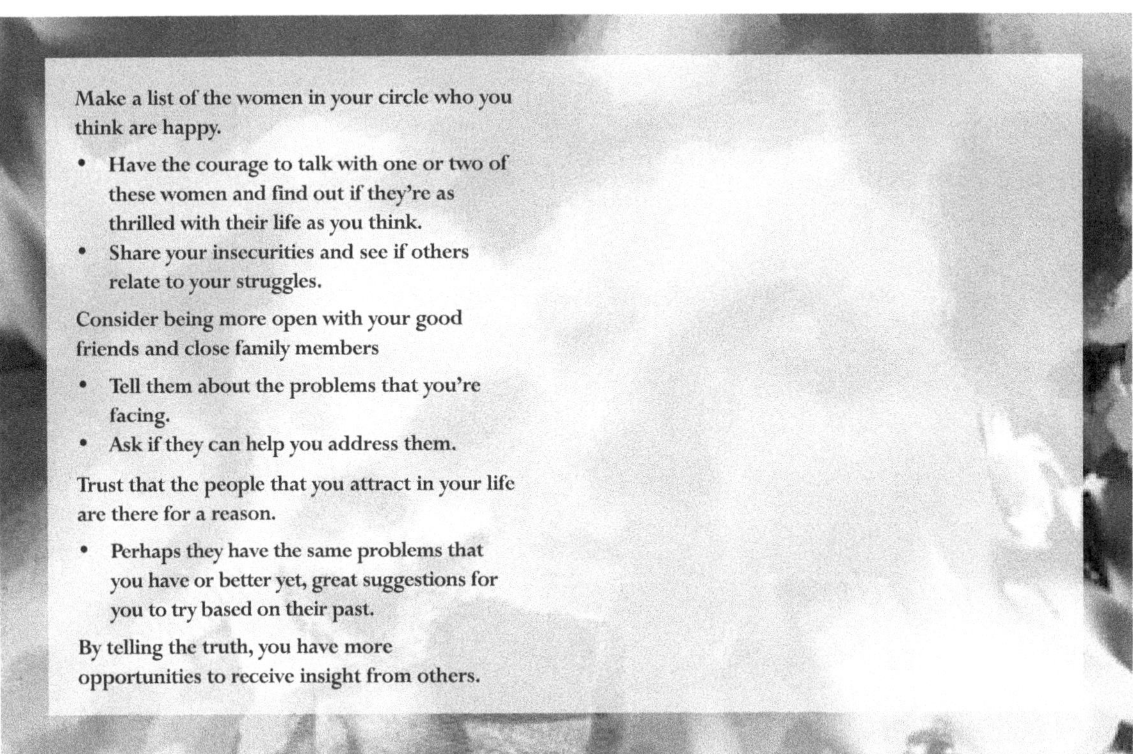

Make a list. . .

Make a list of the women in your circle who you think are happy.

- **Have the courage to talk with one or two of these women and find out if they're as thrilled with their life as you think.**
- **Share your insecurities and see if others relate to your struggles.**

Consider being more open with your good friends and close family members

- **Tell them about the problems that you're facing.**
- **Ask if they can help you address them.**

Trust that the people that you attract in your life are there for a reason.

- **Perhaps they have the same problems that you have or better yet, great suggestions for you to try based on their past.**

By telling the truth, you have more opportunities to receive insight from others.

Tell The Truth, Damn it!

Who do you lie to?
What truth do you need to share?

Use this page to say what you need to say. Write it down. Recite it. Say it fast. Say it slow. Translate it into Hungarian or pig latin. Practice having truths spill from between your lips. Then when you're ready, tell someone.

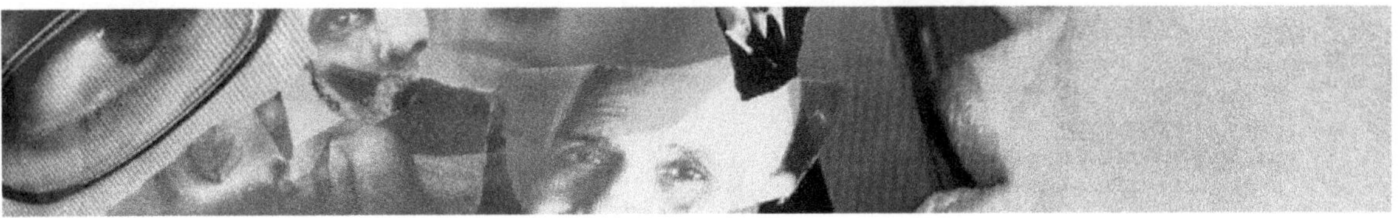

You're Not Alone

Perhaps your truth is too scary. Maybe you've never told anyone before which keeps you from telling someone now. Maybe this secret is holding you back from becoming who you really are. Maybe sharing your secret in a safe way, would make all the difference.

"You are invited to anonymously contribute your secrets to PostSecret. Each secret can be a regret, hope, funny experience, unseen kindness, fantasy, belief, fear, betrayal, erotic desire, feeling, confession, or childhood humiliation. Reveal anything - as long as it is true and you have never shared it with anyone before." ~ *www.postsecret.com*

Be Creative!

On this 4 x 6 postcard below, write your secret, decorate your card and anonymously mail it.

How Does Your Garden Grow?

One spring, my husband and two daughters decided to scatter sunflower seeds along the perimeter of our back fence. I was out front doing other landscaping work at the time, so I wasn't 100 percent sure where the sunflowers had been planted. I'm a big fan of sunflowers and couldn't wait until the end of the summer to see them towering in their bright yellow glory, peeking out over our fence to make their presence known to the world.

Anticipation

I watched lush, green stalks break through the earth and begin their ascent up the slates of our fence. I would point them out to our kids and tell them how beautiful the flowers were going to be. I would remind the kids not to trample on the stalks and talked about how we could use string to secure them to the fence if they needed support.

Confusion

Often times I would look over toward the sunflowers and feel like something wasn't right. I felt that my husband had chosen an odd planting pattern. I would have placed the seeds in a more symmetrical manner. But I brushed the feeling aside, assuming that due to the rain we'd experienced the month prior, some of the seeds simply didn't take. And really, who cares what my flower garden looks like. The real goal was to expose my children to the gardening process.

But something kept nagging at me. I knew sunflowers produce large blooms in late summer and into the fall and that they can grow upwards to twelve feet unless you plant the dwarf version. The leaves of the sunflower are covered in silky hairs that give off a silvery appearance. I couldn't help but notice that the leaves of my sunflowers didn't shimmer in the light and they were smooth to the

PostSecret
13345 Copper Ridge Road
Germantown, Maryland
USA 20874-3454

touch. By mid-August no flower buds had appeared on the large green stalks that were almost taller than the five foot fence, but no where near the height of a soon to be mature sunflower plant.

Investigation

Eventually I walked over to my beautiful sunflowers and inspected them. It turns out that my sunflowers weren't sunflowers at all. They were the biggest damn weeds that I had ever seen! Of course my immediate thought was to pull them, but the optimist in me held out and the next morning, I took my husband to our back window and asked him if those were the sunflowers he had planted.

Verification

"Naw, those are weeds," he said deadpan. "I figured that out a few weeks ago. That's why I kept mentioning that we need to weed the back yard. You really need to pull those out of there." (Apparently the "we" in weeding had nothing to do with he and I and everything to do with me. At least I thought they were sunflowers, whereas he knew that they they weren't but didn't pull them out of the ground.)

Revelation

Had I just listened to my "inner gardener" I would have been able to pull those weeds back in June and maybe the seeds that were planted would have grown and blossomed into something beautiful. All the time I spent "miracle-growing" my flowerbed didn't matter. Instead of fueling the sunflowers, I fueled the weeds that killed them off. When I finally got around to pulling them I realized that in my life, like my garden, I spend too much time cultivating my personal growth instead of removing the weeds so that I can blossom. In fact, I deny that weeds are even there, wasting a lot of time and energy in the process. As a result, my garden can't flourish but instead of realizing that it's due to the weeds, I kid myself into thinking that I simply need to plant better, hardier flowers.

Realization

A master gardener will tell you that weeding is a part of the process. She not only expects weeds, she keeps an eye out for them and gets rid of them on a daily basis. Besides focusing on and being knowledgeable about her plantings, she consistently spends her time and energy removing all that's unnecessary from her garden.

Take a moment and examine your crops. Note what you've been trying to cultivate in your life. If you haven't gotten the yield you've been expecting then perhaps you've been experiencing a little denial yourself. There comes a time when you need to call a weed a weed – and pull it.

Make a list of all the weeds in your life that have taken the form of people, places, things and situations. In other words figure out what is getting in the way of your personal growth. Don't forget to examine yourself for noxious shoots and rogue sproutings, then adopt a master gardener's attitude and anticipate the weeds! Keep an eye out so that you'll not only recognize them, but also pull them immediately. With the weeds out of the way, nature will do the rest for you. Then you can enjoy and appreciate the beauty that surrounds you and fully reap what you sow.

Make a list of all of the weeds in your life. Determine how you might eliminate them from your garden.

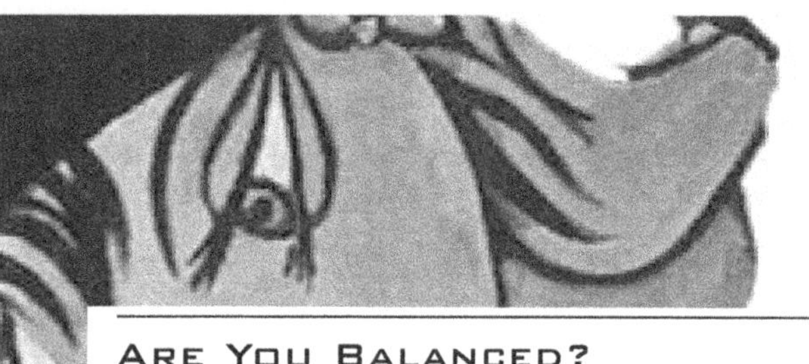

Are You Balanced?

Everyone talks about balance. Whether it's work and home, health and wellness, spending and debt, or relationships and self-love, balance apparently is what it's all about. When you talk about one specific area it makes sense to talk about balance. But when you talk about various conflicting areas, balance can get confusing.

For example, a wonderfully balanced working mom might become completely unhinged if she turned her attention to balancing her finances. What if the day care setup that enables her to best balance work and home is the one thing that is throwing her finances out of whack? Maybe the cheaper day care is located twenty minutes in the opposite direction of her job, which would add to her daily commute, cut into her sleep, prohibit her children from participating in the nighttime activities that keep them balanced and completely screw up her evening routine? What's worse, being relaxed but in debt or having money and stressed to the max?

Being Unbalanced Is Okay

I think most of us simply agree to be unbalanced in some area of our life with the assumption that all will even out at some point. We accept the fact that we can't have it all, – at least not at the same time. Honestly, you can't argue with that logic. The problem is when we assume that creating balance will magically solve all of our problems. As if by creating a balanced life we will eliminate stress all together and continual adjustments will never be necessary.

I had an interesting revelation one Saturday morning watching my daughters, Paige and Jarin, walk across a balance beam at gymnastics class. Jarin ran straight across before jumping off the end with a big smile on her face. She had no fear and never faltered but the Russian judge would have given her a 1.5 for technique because she didn't actually do any of the moves that the instructor had asked for.

Paige on the other hand, took her time and attempted to perform the different poses. She lost her footing, looked much more fearful and pretty much weeble-wabbled all the way across the beam. When she jumped down she looked dejected and disappointed, glancing at me for validation. Like her sister, she did not fall, but unlike her sibling, she at least attempted to perform the moves that the instructor had requested.

Balancing Between Extremes

I think we go back and forth between the two extremes demonstrated by my daughters. Sometimes we rush through what is required and cut corners just to cross items off our "to do" lists. Other times we focus on the quality of our endeavors only to falter anyway and screw the whole thing up.

To the casual observer, Jarin may have seemed like the more balanced child. But if you were really paying attention to the entire practice you would see that she hadn't done the work. Sometimes we come across other balance beam runners in our life, the folks that rush through their day smiling, seemingly footloose and fancy-free. We are in awe of these people and wonder how the hell they do it all yet never seem frazzled. We use them as our measuring stick and allow our misinformed assumptions to give us permission to degrade our own attempts at balance. It's my guess that these folks aren't doing it all and we're just not privy to the stacks of unfinished business piling up in their world.

And we all know the women that falter. They teeter and come close to crashing and burning quite frequently. They have to stop and readjust themselves often and when they do so they look as dejected and unhappy with the results as Paige did with hers. By not bounding across their beam of life, they don't give themselves credit for all the little moves that they have successfully accomplished.

It's Simple: Just Don't Fall

I think to truly be balanced you have to do a little of both. You have to cut corners and not care with the same amount of gusto as when you act conscientiously. In the end, the goal is the same: You are trying not to fall. You do whatever it takes to avoid a massive head injury that will permanently sideline you. Balance is not about perfection as much as it's about knowing when to do the work required and when to sail through exerting as minimal an effort as possible.

I'm sure that eventually my kids will perfect their Saturday morning beam routine. And lucky for them, they are at an age when their only concern is whether or not they lifted their leg and pointed their toe while attempting to make it to the other side. They have no idea then when they get older, the beam will shrink to about half its size and they are going to be handed an egg, a bowling ball, and a chain saw and then be asked to juggle while walking across it.

I hope I'm around to see it. I'll have a good laugh, then I'll compose myself and tell them the secret: If they drop the egg, they can clean it up. If they break the bowling ball, so what? They can buy a new one. But for God's sake, don't drop the chainsaw! Don't cut off your leg trying to keep everything in the air. Stop, turn it off and throw it down! Then I'll encourage them to run to the other side and jump with a big smile on their face. Maybe, just maybe, they'll sprout wings and fly. Or they can simply land on the big ol' gym mat, brush themselves off and try again. Their power comes from not avoiding the beam, but from altering their routine as they see fit.

React. . .

It's simple: just don't fall

Are You An Information Addict?

Be afraid...very afraid. *The Merck Manual of Medical Information* is being aggressively marketed. I first encountered *The Merck Manual* as a newly hired speech pathologist. When I came across a patient with an unfamiliar diagnosis, I would look up the disease to gain insight. Signs and symptoms were laid out in pseudo-English/medical jargon to help me better understand my patients and their recovery course. But a funny thing happened – I started to read it like a New York Times bestseller, convinced that I had every disease known to man. Like a moth to a flame, I was drawn to the book, leisurely reading about illnesses that resulted in black, hairy tongues, rectal bleeding and projectile vomiting, certain that I was a chest x-ray away from an ICU admission.

My Imagination Went Wild

I found myself thinking less about my patients and more about my future life as the girl in the plastic bubble. Would the TV clicker be able to penetrate the latex? Would my husband be allowed to enter for conjugal visits? And most importantly, who would play me in the Lifetime TV movie about my life?

Eventually I was forced to create my own 12-step program to release the book's hold on me. I admitted that I was powerless over medical information. I gave myself over to my lower power, denying that I was capable of contracting anything worse than a hangnail, while convincing myself that I was as immortal as a vampire. I had a co-worker insert a crucifix inside as a bookmark; I replaced the bookends with extra large garlic bulbs and vowed never, I repeat, never to peruse the book again.

Teetering On The Edge

When I quit my job I thought my medical information addiction days were behind me. But as I would browse the women's interest section housed next to the professional healthcare shelves at my local Borders bookstore, I would hear *The Merck Manual* calling to me.

Then the Internet came around and, like a drug dealer,the Web taunted me with its promise of a quick, informational fix. Thousands of medically-based, pharmaceutically-financed Web sites attempted to lure me into their malicious grip with their nifty, online diagnosis software, vitamin supplement recommendations and – horror among horrors – Mapquest directions to my nearest alternative healers. Yes, I'll admit that I do fall off the wagon at times, perusing sites like www.realage.com, but these are for research purposes only out of respect to you, my loyal reader.

But today the unthinkable happened. During my daily www.drphil.com web surfing ritual, as I was reading about some 45-year-old putz that plays X-Box games all day and mooches off of his 75-year-old mommy, a vicious pop-up advertisement got my attention. *The Merck Manual* has been reissued . . . for home use! Redesigned and complete with color diagrams, easy-to-read charts, bullet points and anatomical drawings. It is, and I quote, "Essential for everyone who needs to communicate more affectively with a healthcare professional; understand a medical condition; and learn more about medical terms, procedures and tests." With shaky hands, I clicked on the "Buy Now" button, convinced that I would be unable to afford my addiction, only to see that it sells for a mere $7.99! Quickly, I closed out from the site and immediately began to write this piece to get myself back on track.

You Cannot Change What You Do Not Acknowledge

I know what you're thinking. You're not like me. You can handle it. You enjoy reading medical tidbits for hours on end. You're merely expanding your vocabulary by throwing around words like sternocledomastoid muscle, intubation tray and lupus erythematosus into conversation. You are no health information addict. You can quit at any time.

I know that I cannot cure you of your disease. You must max out your out-of-network deductible and hit rock bottom, before you can climb out from under your health information abyss. I know that you must want to change for you and not for me. Just know that you have been warned.

My work here is done. Besides, I just found a hair in my mouth that I'm pretty sure is attached to something inside my oral cavity. Luckily I've got a tongue scraper in my bathroom with my name on it. God's speed to you all!

Confessions Questions

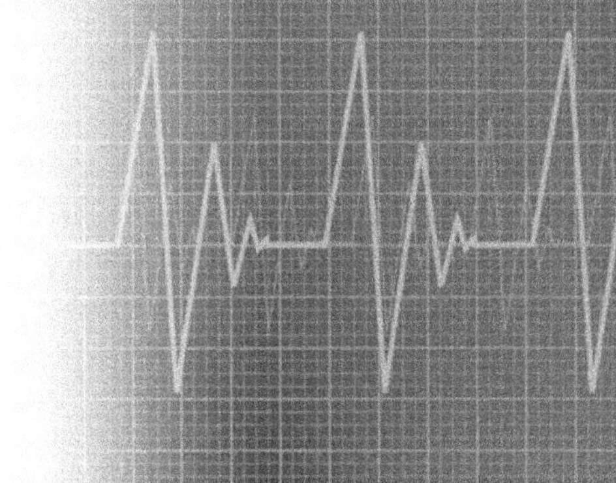

Self-help junkies tend to be health and wellness junkies as well.

What is your biggest health fear? Why?

- *Do you have a family history of this disease?*

- *Have you had this disease before?*

- *Or have you simply heard so much about it that you fear it just in case?*

Do you wait and fight illness or proactively try to create health and wellness?

- *Should you have more faith in your body's ability to stay well?*

- *Is it easier to fear illness instead of doing the work involved to be healthy?*

What Are Your Missing Pieces?

One of the joys of reading to my children is that I get an excuse to rediscover the fabulous works of Shel Silverstein. Books like *The Giving Tree*, *Where the Sidewalk Ends* and *Who Wants A Cheap Rhinoceros?* are not only funny and interesting to kids, but enlightening and entertaining for adults. Although I'm hard pressed to find a Silverstein book that I don't like, I must say that for a self-help junkie, *The Missing Piece* is a definite must read.

A cute little circle with an empty space shaped like a slice of pie, rolls around the landscape in search of his missing piece. Because his piece is missing, he can't roll so fast and has plenty of time to stop and play with a beetle or allow a butterfly to land on his head. Excited about the prospects of finding a piece to complete him, he happily sings:

> ***"Oh I'm lookin' for my missin' piece***
> ***I'm lookin' for my missin' piece***
> ***Hi-dee-ho, here I go,***
> ***Lookin' for my missin' piece."***

We're All On The Look Out

Like the circle, we all search for our missing piece, but usually we are not as jovial. Instead of happily searching for what we need, we tend to desperately seek it out, convinced that it's the missing piece that will bring us joy.

Throughout the book the circle comes across various pieces that don't quite fit, crushes one piece from clinging too tightly and loses one because he doesn't hold on tight enough. Some pieces don't want to be "his" missing piece. Others are happy to oblige.

Eventually he finds his missing piece and becomes a complete circle. With his edges uniformly curved and seamless, he rolls with reckless abandon, passing by the beetles and butterflies that he used to stop and frolic with. So full and encompassing, he can't even sing his theme song anymore without sounding like he has a mouthful of marbles. Soon he realizes that perhaps the journey was more fun than the destination and releases his glorious piece so as to slow down and enjoy the delights of his day once again.

Our Missing Pieces Make Us Unique

Recently as I read the story it struck me that perhaps it is best to honor our missing pieces. Sure others might view them as eccentricities or flaws, but these are the things that make us unique. It is our missing pieces that allow us to create goals, expand our horizons and experience new things.

Some pieces, of course, need to be found. Most people want solutions to problems rather than unfinished business hanging over their heads. Sometimes it's simply the calm that comes with a decision rather than the chosen course of action that gives us the serenity that we are searching for. But often the problem with finding missing pieces is that we do not take the time to honor what we've achieved.

I've notice that many people have shifted their focus from maintaining to concentrating solely on gaining.

Compliment any homeowner on her beautiful new living room furniture and she's sure to point out how she plans on painting the walls, recarpeting the floors and saving up for a plasma television. A year later when you compliment her on the new carpet, wall color and the kick ass TV you're watching, she's sure to share with you how dated her kitchen now looks and the new appliances and granite counter tops she needs to invest in.

It is our missing pieces that allow us to create goals, expand our horizons and experience new things.

Besides driving ourselves crazy we allow others to project their insanity onto us. Bring that same special someone to enough family functions and everyone will want to know when you're getting engaged. Once you get engaged, all talk turns to the wedding plans. There at the fire hall, as you dance the tarantella with yet another drunk relative, the "When are you going to have a baby?" interrogation starts. As soon as you announce your pregnancy, everyone wants to know, "What sex? What names have you picked?" Then while you're sitting on an inflated plastic doughnut waiting for your episiotomy to heal, someone will inevitably ask when you will be returning to work.

Are We Just Born This Way?

As a nation we Americans have such a go, go, go mindset that we have no clue when we should slow down and stop trying to claim the next big thing in our lives. On the one hand, it's what makes our country great because the truth is we've accomplished a hell of a lot since 1776. There are other countries that have been around for thousands of years that haven't come close to what we've accomplished from an industrial, technological or medical standpoint.

Besides having a history of being on the go, science has proven that over time our brains become re-wired to not only keep up with a quickening pace, but to expect it. Just for laughs find a rotary phone and use it for a day. Dial a phone number with a "9" in it a few times and note how your head almost explodes from impatience. In the time it takes for the dial to rotate back from 9 to 0, you could manually punch in a phone number (area code included) on a touch-tone phone.

When you constantly give yourself over to the fast-paced, results-oriented world that we inhabit, it becomes difficult to pull yourself back from the edge. Frankly, I can understand why the circle from Silverstein's book wanted to drop his perfect piece and take it easy for a while. His gaping hole gave him an excuse to slow down and literally smell the roses. Just as a bout with the flu gives you a reason to miss work or a crisis at home allows you to pass on an evening out, we all secretly relish opportunities to give in to our imperfections and be honest about them as well. But the difference between my circle friend and most of us is that he consciously chose to be imperfect and didn't wait for a breakdown in vitality or mental health to require his transformation. He not only embraced his imperfections, he understood how in fact they served him.

Be Thankful for Your Missing Piece

It's easy to give thanks to the universe for abundance and blessings. Perhaps you should also take a moment and give thanks for all of your missing pieces. Be grateful for unmet goals, imperfect body parts, incomplete home repair projects and looming deadlines. Remember, unfinished business not only allows you the luxury of reflection but also the opportunity to change your mind.

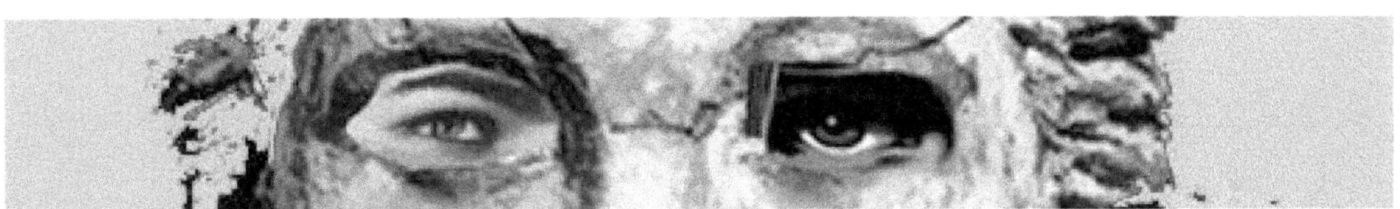

Maybe those thighs you hate aren't responding to your exercise regimen because they need to lift weights rather than only walking on a treadmill each day. Perhaps the reason you can't find the perfect wallpaper pattern is because you're supposed to paint that wall instead. What if the frustration you're feeling about living in a pig pen is less about your inability to afford a cleaning lady and more about your children needing to be assigned extra chores? And maybe your boss isn't an idiot and you need a new place of employment instead? Or maybe everything is fine as is and you just need to stop putting so much pressure on yourself to be perfect.

As you review all the pieces that make up the whole that is your life, take a moment to honor that parts not yet present and accounted for. View these gaping holes as opportunities to make different, perhaps more appropriate choices. Better yet, give yourself permission to do nothing and simply sit in them for a while. Become comfortable with the empty space and get to know it intimately before you try to fill it. Maybe, this level of trust and patience has been the missing piece all along.

React. . .

How To Be Courageous?

Often my excuses for not doing things have been valid, like when I didn't have the time, money or know-how. I'm okay with that. What I am ashamed of is all of the times that I didn't have the courage. I think I had it once. I'm wondering where has it gone?

Finding Yourself

Elizabeth Berg, in her novel *The Pull of the Moon*, illustrates the loss of courage beautifully. The main character, Nan, turns fifty and decides that she must find herself before she can embrace menopause and live her remaining years contently. So she takes off to places unknown on a self-discovery road trip. Tapping into her feminine wisdom, she follows no agenda or timetable and decides instead to follow the pull of the moon. Her journal entries and letters to the husband she's left behind make up the entire book.

One passage in particular caught my attention. In it, Nan writes about her childhood desires. She would read Hitchcock and then daydream about how someday she would be a famous writer. After looking through her treasure box of found objects - bird's nests, stones, dried flowers - she imagined herself as an archeologist, setting out into the world to make amazing discoveries. Once her homework was completed each night she would visualize her future life as a beloved and respected teacher, inspiring the minds of her students.

It never occurred to the childhood Nan that she wouldn't make her dreams come true or become the person she was imagining. Nan recalls the moment when her courage began to waiver:

Then at night, before I went to sleep, I'd read teen magazines, which I'd just discovered. I read about where hems should fall and how faces should look and what to say to boys to lure them and hold them. And I thought, wait. I don't think that I can be this. It began to occur to me that I was a failure. I lost my grip. By the middle of the year, the phone replaced Hitchcock and my sure dreams of being everything. On my dresser, tubes of pink and coral lipstick and sable-brown mascara appeared, blemish creams, concealer. Concealer, yes. The rocks in my closet got lost, and so did I.

Reading that passage blew me away! I never made that connection before. I used to lose myself in Nancy Drew Mysteries, but, like Nan, I eventually replaced reading *The Mystery of the 99 Steps* with desperately following the steps dictated to me by the writers of *Teen Magazine*.

The pre-teen boys I knew at that time were trading baseball cards and pretending to win the World Series in their backyards. Yet I would man right-center field during my softball games, wondering if my pony-tail looked cute under my ball cap and if my ugly orange uniform was giving me a "farmers tan."

I think we lose our pre-teen innocence the moment that we gain the skill required to masterfully apply lip-gloss, and then the "how to's" never stop. We're instructed on how to get a date, lose ten pounds and pick a bathing suit for our body type. Then we advance to how to get into college and decorate our dorm rooms on a budget,

. . .recapture the piece of yourself that you have left behind.

only to graduate to how to get jobs and go from the office to evening with one outfit and a change of eye shadow. Eventually we are being told how to snag a husband, get pregnant, make wrapping paper from recycled Tampax boxes, feng shui our bathrooms and juggle work, home and children while having great sex lives.

I'm worried. As the baby boomers age (and advertisers continue to market their products to them) I fear that the "how to's" will keep coming. I bet you my life savings that someday right beside *Seventeen Magazine* there will be a copy of *Seventy Magazine* telling women how to decoupage their walkers and pick up men in nursing homes. Bejeweled coverings for colostomy bags will be all the rage, and women will be discussing whether or not to wear their casual or dress dentures out to dinner.

Obviously, tips and techniques can be helpful. But constantly following the "how to's" of others takes less courage than figuring it out as you go along.

We know that all of these "how to's" are just guidelines. But if we allow them to guide us completely we run the risk of losing a part of our authentic self along the way. So I have no "how to's" to share with you. I'm not sure what you need to do to recapture the piece of yourself that you have left behind. However, I believe it is important to pinpoint the moment when the girl in you decided that she couldn't become the woman she wanted to be. If you can find enough courage to explore that for a while, then perhaps you'll have enough left over to find her and release her from where she has been hiding all this time. I'll bet she has some wisdom to share. Have the courage to listen and learn.

Confession Questions:

Can you pinpoint the exact moment when you lost your confidence and started looking outside of yourself for the answers?

What do you remember loving to do as a child? What were your favorite books, hobbies, activities, foods, music, movies, and television shows? Did you keep a diary? What did you write about?

Close your eyes, play a song from those years. Go there. What do you see?

. . . punishing yourself for all of your faults

SELF CORRECT

Self Correct 1 a : to make or set right : AMEND b : COUNTERACT, NEUTRALIZE c : to alter or adjust so as to bring to some standard or required condition : 2 a : to punish with a view to reforming or improving b : to point out usually for amendment the errors or faults of

If you are a self-help junkie you're probably a master at the second definition, *punishing yourself for all of your faults.* Allow me to also go out on a limb and suggest that you might be a tad obsessive about the *altering and adjusting* part as well.

Perhaps it's the search for an easy answer or a simple solution that keeps you from mastering the art of self-help. Regardless, the following essays are to stimulate your thinking and bring into your consciousness ways to successfully create the permanent positive changes that you've been trying to achieve.

CONFIDENCE

Once you feel worthy, you will hold yourself in higher esteem and, by default, you will feel more confident.

Confidence Versus Knowledge

When I do research, I like to start by looking up the dictionary definition of the term I'm investigating. Merriam Webster defines confidence as: a feeling or consciousness of one's powers or a reliance on one's circumstances; faith or belief that one will act in a right, proper or effective way; the quality or state of being certain.

Personally, I'm confident in my ability to manage money, but when it comes to financial planning I doubt my abilities. I don't understand the stock market although my husband has explained it to me a thousand times. When I hear about the Dow Jones Industrial Average, I immediately think of Hugh Downs and wonder what he's been up to since leaving ABC's 20/20.

I believe that my lack of confidence in this subject is due to my lack of experience. My husband enjoys financial planning so that's his thing. I like simple math, so I keep tabs on our checkbook. But if I had to take over this aspect of our finances, I know that I'm smart enough to figure it out. Therefore, don't confuse confidence with having a skill set. I'm talking about the big picture here, as in having the confidence in yourself to create the life that you desire. But how do you become confident enough to reach for the brass ring and then maintain it when faced with adversity?

Mixed Messages

The self-help boom of the 1990's gave women strategies to be as confident as possible. We were taught to focus on our true selves and were asked to determine our passions. Operating from a place of authenticity was supposed to set us up for success, not failure. If we focused on our skills, what we were really good at doing, failure would not be an option. This was empowering unless we actually became successful. Then our assertiveness was viewed as aggressiveness, and we women were characterized as bitchy.

So, in order to be accepted and supported for the long term we adapted, and learned to package confidence along with compassion and humbleness. If we got too cocky, the world would gleefully await our downfall. Think Martha Stewart, Madonna, Rosie O'Donnell, Britney Spears, Mariah Carey, Oprah Winfrey – you get my drift. This may explain why confidence is such a difficult trait to obtain. It changes our reality, which may change the way others feel about us.

Change the Wording

The confidence gurus must have sensed this inequity when it came to successful women and their low levels of self-assuredness because they eventually changed the wording and started targeting our self-esteem. By focusing on the self, confidence building got a boost. We were encouraged to listen to our inner voice, write feeling letters, affirm our beliefs about ourselves and embrace the power of positive thinking.

At a glance these techniques were great ideas. Create confidence from the inside out by teaching us how to dip into our self-esteem well and use it to our advantage. But there was one problem. The more we examined our lives, the more faults and discrepancies we uncovered. Our attempts to be more confident just made us adept at walking the earth, feeling inadequate.

The Problem With Self-Esteem

My research on confidence led me to The National Association For Self-Esteem (NASE). NASE specifically states that self-esteem and confidence are not the same. By definition, self-esteem requires being confident in yourself while also feeling worthy of all that you obtain and achieve.

Whoa! Hold the phone! Aren't confidence and self-esteem synonymous with one another? Quickly, I ran to the dictionary and verified that self-esteem does in fact mean: a confidence and satisfaction in oneself. But if the NASE people are correct, it would certainly explain why creating confidence feels like such an up-hill battle. If you don't feel *worthy* of the skills that you inherently possess, then you won't feel confident in using your abilities as needed. So I looked up the word worthy and read: it is that which has value. Interesting.

Confidence Is A Process

You must start by acknowledging the valuable skills and abilities that you have. When you recognize these traits in yourself, then, and only then, will you begin to feel worthy. Once you feel worthy, you will hold yourself in higher esteem and, by default, you will feel more confident.

Confidence as it turns out, is an end result, not a starting point. When you understand that you add value by performing the skills that you inherently possess and sharing your gifts, eventually you will become confident. This newfound confidence will then propel you forward and give you the guts to try new things, make necessary changes in your life, and meet goals.

What the hell…give it a try and see.

What the hell . . . give it a try and see

Make a list of **100** different skills/talents that you possess. (use the sheet provided on the next page)

- Yes, you do have 100 skills. Can you tie your shoes? Whistle? Walk while chewing gum? See what I mean? Maybe you're a good cake baker and a great listener. Just brag about yourself on paper and embrace all that you do well.

Review your list and note specifically how your skills add value to your life and to the lives of others.

- Baking a birthday cake for a co-worker adds value to the work environment by building a sense of community. Many people can bake a cake, but going out of your way to recognize someone's birthday speaks to the type of person you are. You are thoughtful and kind – you are valuable.

By recognizing your value, you honor the fact that you have worth.

- Be proud of who you are and what you do by not brushing off compliments or downplaying your contributions.
- For example, your choice to share your kindness and culinary skills makes a statement. By being authentic, you honor yourself.

Review your list and identify skills that you hide from others or minimize.

- Why do you do this?
- What are you afraid of?
- What would happen if people saw the "real" you?

Build up your confidence.

- Start sharing your gifts with others.
- Since you'll officially become confident when you are conscious of your power, begin to rely on your abilities and become certain of your skills.

Don't confuse confidence with having a skill set.

- You may need different skills in the future in order to create change in your life.
- Be confident in your ability to learn something new, react appropriately and adjust as needed as you meet goals and create the life that you desire and deserve.

What gets in your way? What blocks you from achieving your goals? What nasty comments do you say to yourself over and over again?

1.__________
2.__________
3.__________
4.__________
5.__________
6.__________
7.__________
8.__________
9.__________
10.__________
11.__________
12.__________
13.__________
14.__________
15.__________
16.__________
17.__________
18.__________
19.__________
20.__________
21.__________
22.__________
23.__________
24.__________
25.__________
26.__________
27.__________
28.__________
29.__________
30.__________
31.__________
32.__________
33.__________
34.__________
35.__________
36.__________
37.__________
38.__________
39.__________
40.__________
41.__________
42.__________
43.__________
44.__________
45.__________
46.__________
47.__________
48.__________
49.__________
50.__________
51.__________
52.__________
53.__________
54.__________
55.__________
56.__________
57.__________
58.__________
59.__________
60.__________
61.__________
62.__________
63.__________
64.__________
65.__________
66.__________
67.__________
68.__________
69.__________
70.__________
71.__________
72.__________
73.__________
74.__________
75.__________
76.__________
77.__________
78.__________
79.__________
80.__________
81.__________
82.__________
83.__________
84.__________
85.__________
86.__________
87.__________
88.__________
89.__________
90.__________
91.__________
92.__________
93.__________
94.__________
95.__________
96.__________
97.__________
98.__________
99.__________
100.__________

The Simple Life

Nowadays, being referred to as a simpleton could be taken as a compliment. Books about simple living line our shelves. *Real Simple* magazine has a prominent perch at the checkout line in the grocery store, and simple living groups meet to discuss ways to unclutter their lives. People from all walks of life are seeking ways to simplify their day-to-day existence.

Grandma DelBene (my husband's maternal grandmother) was simple. She was simple as in smart, unadulterated and pure. Prior to her death at 85 she made a mean homemade gnocchi and brought a level of calmness and clarity with her whenever she entered a room. She was a lovely woman. Cuddly soft with a striking mane of white hair that shined like a halo atop her head, she was the quiet yet quintessential matriarch of my husband's extended family.

I was always quite fascinated with Grandma. Content to silently sit on the sidelines, she had struck me as a woman that knew things, intuitively. She exuded serenity and wisdom that only time and observation can bring forth. Being fortunate to have access to this wise woman elder, I wanted to learn her secrets and more about her life. So a few years before her death I had the pleasure of interviewing her. At times, it was like pulling teeth. Simple people tend to have simple answers. For example:

What did you think about America when you first came here from Italy?
"It was nice."
Were you scared?
"No. I was glad to be here and living with my father."
What did you admire most about your husband?
"The way he loved his children."
What advice would you give to a woman that was about to get married?
"Make sure that you're friends and never go to bed mad."
What was your favorite time period?
"The 1950's because we got more things [gadgets] that made life easier in the kitchen."

Although she felt that the world had gotten rather complicated, she sure did like having a microwave and a television. When it came to her interpersonal skills, she kept it simple as well.

Grandma, you tend to have very interesting opinions on things, but I've noticed that you never share them unless you are specifically asked. Why is that?
"Growing up my mother made it clear that I should be seen and not heard. So I guess I've just always been that way."
I've also noticed that you never say anything bad about anyone. If people are gossiping, you never chime in.
"Yep."
Well, what kind of people don't you like?
"People that think they know everything. I ignore people who think that they know it all."
So what do you do if you're stuck in a room with someone like that?
"I think about other things, like what I need to do around the house or what I want to cook."

Over the years, I noticed that she managed to maintain a life that was simple and free of complications. She avoided drama by practicing the following tenets:

If you don't have anything nice to say, don't say anything at all. During the sixteen years that I knew her, I never heard her utter a negative remark, about anyone. Her family attested to the fact that she always maintained a no-gossip policy.

If someone wants your opinion, they'll ask for it. She rarely interjected her opinions into conversations. To the observer, it appeared that she did not have any. But if you took the time to engage her, she would tell you exactly how she felt without attempting to shape your own opinion. With her, you got to have a conversation, not a confrontation, which is why I enjoyed talking with her.

Don't stick your nose where it doesn't belong. Even when it came to family controversy, she kept it simple, choosing to never meddle in the affairs of her children. Take "The Great Bowling Ball Incident of 1966." My father-in-law, Joe, was bowling seven nights a week. My mother-in-law, Lulu, got fed up, so she took the bowling ball and hid it in Grandma's basement, a dangerous place with low ceilings, limited light and everything Grandma ever owned that didn't fit in her equally dangerous attic space. When Joe showed up looking for his ball and his wife (sadly, in that order), you'd assume that Grandma would take her daughter's side. Not so.

"Joe, your bowling ball is in the basement. Go get it and the two of you get the hell out of my house 'cause I don't want to know about your marriage," was the extent of her involvement.

Be Compassionate. Throughout her lifetime she cared for the sick, and volunteered at church and her local hospital. She helped out because it was the right thing to do, not to make herself look better. And she offered her help to anyone, regardless of the circumstances that got them in a bind in the first place. She's the type of woman that you could tell anything to and she would still love you, warts and all.

Do for Yourself. Although she quit school after the 8th grade, she read everything she could get her hands on, educating herself in the process. She was a working mother before it was hip, successfully raised four children and continued to support herself after her husband passed away. Until her death, she lived with her eldest daughter and accepted help as needed, but even in her later years she attempted to do for herself as often as possible.

Family Is Important
She died the day after Christmas in 2004. That was the only Christmas that she didn't host a holiday dinner or provide a bounty of homemade foods to her family. Until the end she spent her spare time crocheting beautiful afghans to pass down to her great-grandchildren. She quietly and without great fanfare worked hard, loved well and in the process created a family that continues in that tradition. No, there will probably never be a stamp commemorated in her honor, but to those whose lives she touched, she certainly made an impression.

The Secret to the Simple Life
When I started my interview, I was searching for her secrets. I wanted to know what made this fine, loving woman tick, so to speak. What I discovered was that her secret was in *not* believing that she knew the secret. And that's when it all became clear to me. The key to the simple life that many of us are searching for is accepting that we don't have all of the answers. Our only requirement is to have our own

answers and live accordingly rather than expending so much energy judging and criticizing the lives of others.

The World Is A Complicated Place

We are living in a very complicated time. Technology, politics, religion, world events, lifestyle debates, and financial concerns are just a few of the hot topics that are vying for our attention right now. And although I too am glad to have a microwave and a television, there are times when I listen to the stories of the Grandma DelBene's of the world and wistfully yearn for a simpler era. Not that their lives were without struggle or complexity. But they seemed to be more content with simpler outcomes.

Life will never be simple. It always has been and always will be complicated. Maybe the more appropriate goal is not to simplify our lives, but to simplify our expectations. The Serenity Prayer asks for the serenity to accept what we cannot change and the courage to change what we can. Perhaps the true key to the simple life is the prayer's third request; the wisdom to know the difference.

Life will never be simple. It always has been and always will be complicated. Maybe the more appropriate goal is not to simplify our lives, but to simplify our expectations.

Although age and life experience can be your ally, some people, like Grandma, seemed to be blessed with this insight early on. She always had the wisdom to know the difference. This was not only her secret but the gift that she possessed. And like the afghans she made for my daughters, I was lovingly warmed by her wisdom and blanketed by her grace.

I hope that you have a Grandma DelBene in your life. If you don't, I'm sure that somewhere there is a wise, elderly woman with a story to tell that may reveal many insights. Someone content to be seen and not heard, but secretly hoping that perhaps you'll ask anyway. So pull up a chair and sit and visit for a while. For sometimes the path to your own simple truth can be via a walk down another's memory lane.

Seeing The Signs

"You will know what you need to know, when you need to know it." ~ Joseph Aldo

Joseph Aldo, an intuitive who spoke at the Institute of Integrative Nutrition, stated the above sentence near the end of my health-counseling coursework. I don't mean to brag, but upon hearing this sentence I had my first and only "A-Ha Moment". You know, the moment of clarity one gets while watching Oprah.

It was a remarkable statement. What if, like Dorothy and her ruby slippers, (Oprah's favorite metaphor, by the way), we have what we require to succeed all along? A feeling of serenity washed over me as I realized I already had all of the answers I would ever need. The key was understanding that I would simply tap into this information when it was required and not a moment before. This was in stark contrast to my previous understanding of life. I had erroneously believed the answer was out there, somewhere, rather than inside. Because of this, I spent precious time, energy and resources searching for information outside of myself.

When I finally began to live the above quote, life began to fall into place. Note the emphasis on the word, began. It didn't fall into place and stay there. Life did not suddenly become perfect and completely manageable. Rather I began to trust my life and release my death grip on outcomes and measurable deliverables.

How The Universe Works

For example, a few years ago I wanted to design a Web site for my business, but I couldn't afford to hire a professional. A friend suggested that I barter by offering my skills in exchange for another's Web design expertise. But I had nothing to offer. The only skill set that I had was my previous experience working as a speech therapist, but since doing nothing would get me nowhere, I logged on to the e-mail based support group for my counseling course and offered to trade speech therapy services for help in designing my homepage.

The odds of finding a Web master with a lingering speech impediment were slim to none, but since you must ask the universe specifically for what you need if you're ever going to get it, I figured, what the hell…and went for it.

The following morning, Kristin, a gal from my class who I hardly knew, approached me.

"Are you a speech therapist?" she asked.

"Yea," I said.

"I need to find a good speech therapist in Brooklyn and I was wondering if you knew of any or a Web site where I could search for therapists close to my apartment," she

I trust that all will be revealed to me in time. I believe that I'm part of a big plan that I can't possibly understand at this very moment.

continued. "You see, I've had a slight speech problem since I was child and I think it's time that I try to fix it," she explained.

For a second I just stared at her. How weird that out of the blue someone I didn't know would ask me about speech therapy.

"I know this is going to sound like an odd question," I said, "but do you by chance know anything about Web design?"

"Actually, that's what I do for a living," she replied.

"You're kidding me! Last night I posted a message to the e-group that said I was looking to trade speech therapy services for Web design help," I stated.

"I haven't checked my e-mail in a few days, I just remembered that you used to work as a speech therapist," she replied in disbelief.

I'd heard a million times before that if you tell the universe what you need, you will be provided for and I believe that to be true. I mean, I've never gone hungry or been homeless. My family moved from Pittsburgh to Manhattan, took a pay cut, started paying quadruple for just about everything from rent to food to parking and yet we always had enough to pay the bills. I knew that the universe was taking care of things, but when a Web designer that I barely knew just happened to request speech therapy only 12 hours after I offered my services, well that was absolutely amazing to me!

Kristin made an appointment to visit me at my apartment for a speech evaluation. The morning of our scheduled meeting time I was nervous. I hadn't evaluated anyone's speech in four years and didn't have any tests with me. I had called an old co-worker and asked her to send me a few materials, but they hadn't arrived. So once again, I repeated my mantra of knowing when I needed to know, took a deep breath and stopped worrying. Approximately two hours before the evaluation, the testing materials I had requested arrived in the mail.

When Kristin arrived, I did an oral motor exam, tested her for apraxia and then settled in to learn more about what had triggered her speech problem in the first place. Right on my shelf was the perfect book to help her deal with the personal issues of her past that had caused her to clench her teeth and create the speech troubles that started when she was four years old.

Besides giving Kristin exercises to retrain her mouth and tongue, we discussed the emotional and spiritual issues that she needed to focus on. The information that helped her most was not information that I could have prepared ahead of time. It was only through listening to her story and trusting the process that I figured out how to help her. In essence, I conducted my first ever, holistic speech therapy session and it was a lot of fun.

Kristin's speech distortions began to go away and we met frequently to shape my Web site in terms of text and content. But when it was time to actually create and upload the site to a server, Kristin was too busy and suggested that I contact someone different. Again I asked the universe for help and found a web designer, Tom, located in Israel, who could create an entire site for me for less than $300. Because of my initial work with Kristin, I was able to give Tom my text and Web ideas. I merely told him that I liked the color blue and was into moon symbols. Within days my site was finished, looking exactly as I had imagined and was ready to go live.

It Is All About Trust

Trusting that I will be privy to information when needed has made all the difference. It is through this trust that I am able to operate in the world. Don't misunderstand. I still stress out and yell at my kids and act like a bitch toward my husband, and take things personally, and speak out of turn, and make mistakes, and worry about the future, and question myself, and cry and want help from others, and seek out advice, and lean on my friends and family, and wonder what I should do next. But I do it less often and without as much fear and confusion. I trust that all will be revealed to me in time. I believe that I'm part of a big plan that I can't possibly understand at this very moment. I see failures as lessons learned and keep moving.

Because of this concept I wrote my newsletter for three years and assumed that the women receiving it needed the information I was providing. Similarly, I trust that you will benefit from one of the following random quotes, comments and viewpoints. They are left here for you to peruse and be inspired by based on what your needs are right now. Pick the one that resonates most with you at this very moment and then write about it in the space provided.

"Life is good. Do what you like. Like what you do." ~ Quote on my coffee mug bought from www.lifeisgood.com

"If you put one foot into yesterday and the other foot into tomorrow – you'll shit all over today." ~ My mother, Micki's favorite thing to say when giving me advice.

"I know I'm not worthy, but I get up every day and God willing he will give me his grace and make me worthy." ~ Quote from a old friend that is now extremely religious. It seems as though the more religious she becomes the less worthy she becomes. This I do not understand at all.

"Yes. When the Pope is a black, hispanic lesbian – and they change the music." ~ My uncle, an ex-priest, answering the question as to whether he would return to the priesthood if they allowed married priests to serve.

"The longer I'm married to you, the more I understand divorce – and lesbianism." ~ The best one-liner I ever uttered during a fight with my husband. I have never topped it.

It's called the curse of the capable woman. If you're too needy you'd never be able to handle his leaving week after week. So you become extremely capable only to find that no one, including your husband, offers any help because they assume you have everything under control. It's a vicious cycle. A nasty catch 22. ~ One of my best friends, Cindy, explaining what happens to women that marry work-a-holic men who frequently travel.

"No more conflama!" A slang term that describes what happens when conflict and drama collide. ~ www.urbandictionary.com

Setting Intentions For Change

In Gary Zukav's book, *The Seat of The Soul*, he talks in depth about intentions. He postulates that the universe honors intentions but not necessarily the results of intentions. In other words, if your good intention goes bad, no points are deducted from your karmic scorecard. (Like when you ask a woman when her baby is due only to find out she's not pregnant. OUCH! Hey, you meant well, didn't you?)

Usually we are taught that a negative outcome is telling us that we need to DO something different. However, Zukav suggests that it's more efficient to THINK something different. Instead of reworking various scenarios in your head, you can reflect on your intentions, determine if they are from a place of truth and work from there.

If your goal is to improve a relationship with your partner that you continuously fight with, look objectively at your situation. You may see that you exert too many rules and ultimatums while operating from an "I'll show him/her" perspective. Zukav would tell you to take an honest inventory of your thoughts. You may discover that you were trying to control the person, which would explain the breakdown in communication. He would suggest that you change your intention and make it to better connect with this person. Then you can focus on your listening skills, your level of empathy and your own actions, which you can, in fact, control. Working in this manner can bring about a breakthrough and create change. But the actions required are more inwardly focused.

Use the space below to write about the ways in which you should "think" differently.

The Two Most Powerful Words

Everything ever created started with an idea. For example the telephone didn't just pop onto our kitchen counters. Alexander Graham Bell had the idea to electronically transmit speech at the age of 18. It took eleven years for him to successfully transmit his voice to his assistant, Mr. Watson. In essence, his initial thought transferred into an action, which resulted in an outcome.

The Power of Thought

The book *Conversations with God*, by Neale Donald Walsch talks about the power of thought as a creative force that shapes reality. Since every outcome starts with a thought, the best way to change an outcome is to change the thought that precedes it. Because of this, the most powerful creative words are simply, I AM.

Often times when we are frustrated, we say to our friends, "I don't understand why I can't change. I want to be happy, lose weight, change jobs, get married, or get organized. Why can't I achieve my goals?"

Yet if you say you want to lose weight, you are in fact achieving this goal. You are – wanting to lose weight – thus not actually losing any. In essence you create a reality that consists of wanting rather than obtaining or achieving. If you say, "I will lose weight," again, you create a reality that occurs at some point in the future. But if you change the phrase to, "I am losing weight," then the reality you create is one that lines up with the goal that you've set.

Isn't That Cheating?

I know what you're thinking, it's dishonest to say that you are losing weight until you step on the scale and see the numbers getting smaller. Just saying it doesn't make it so. Yet if you attempt to lose weight by eating more vegetables, exercising until you sweat, drinking more water, ingesting smaller portions, and only eating when hungry you probably tell people that you're trying to lose weight. Or worse yet, you don't say anything at all and hope that someone else notices your changing exterior. But certainly you don't wait until you start to lose to actually do all of the above steps. Both happen simultaneously.

If you do the above steps and your body does not get smaller, you can abandon the process without much guilt because, hey, you can try again tomorrow. Trying doesn't require that you to make any special promises to yourself. Whereas if you state out loud that you are in fact losing weight, you force yourself without a lot of drama to do the things necessary to achieve the goal. You naturally participate in actions that are in line with your intentions.

Keeping It Real

This doesn't mean that you can eat a dozen doughnuts while chanting, "I am losing weight, I am losing weight." That makes you a liar and little insane. Instead, write it

. . . then the reality you create is one that lines up with the goal that you've set.

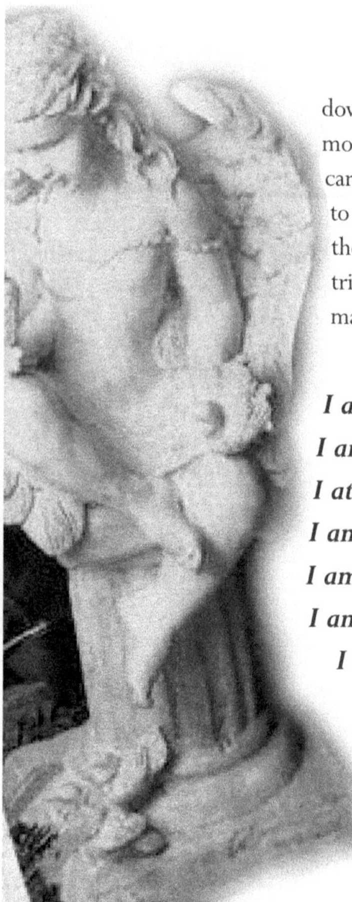

down twenty-five times each morning. Repeat this mantra in the car while you drive to work. Say it to yourself while you wait in line at the dry cleaners. Do this not out of trickery, but because it helps to make your goals a part of your reality, and will subconsciously help you to make choices that best reflect this reality.

In this spirit of positive, proactive change, let me share with you the power of positive affirmations. If you want to join me (say, I am joining you, to yourself), here are some affirmations to get you started:

I am healthy and fit.
I am a strong and powerful woman.
I attract money to me when I need it.
I am eating nutritious foods.
I am moving my body daily.
I am successful.
I am a worthy of taking time for myself.
I am capable of handling difficult situations.
I am in tune to the wisdom of my body.

And just for fun…
I am woman
hear me roar.
I'm Henry the 8th, I
am, I am!
I am made of rubber
and you're made of
glue, everything you
say bounces off of me
and sticks to you.

And just in case this actually works…
I am the owner of perky and firm boobs.
I am a multiple orgasm magnet
I am a lottery winner.
I am starting a new trend: Tattoos are out -
Stretch marks are in!

Write Your Own:

THE "RIGHT NOW" DISEASE

I grew up out in the sticks. To this day my parents cannot get cable, call waiting or a decent cell phone signal. Out in the boonies we used well water, which meant that we could not run the dishwasher, wash clothes or take a shower at the same time. When our power went out, we had to wait until the lights came back on to flush because our toilet ran on an electric pump. This created quite a stench with four people in the family. Growing up where I did taught me much about waiting.

Waiting Is for Wimps

Most people download information from the Internet instead of driving to the library, send faxes in place of mailed letters and view digital pictures off their camera moments after taking the shot. Even my parents have a gas fireplace that operates with a remote control! Apparently only a sucker waits for things anymore.

So when I think about change and what makes it so darn difficult, I can't help but wonder if it has something to do with our inability to wait. Our culture is so accustomed to speedy services and timely results that we associate waiting as a failure on some level. We have been subtly retrained to believe that efficiency is better than effectiveness. We'll eat a lousy tasting pizza and tell ourselves that it is okay because it arrived on our doorstep within thirty minutes of hanging up the phone.

No wonder we breathe heavy sighs of annoyance when results are not swift.

The infomercial arena has made billions feeding off our hatred of waiting. We spend tons of money on cookware that guarantees a three-course dinner from one pot in half the time, diet products that promise weight loss in mere days and solutions that will remove five decades of rust in one dip. No wonder we breathe heavy sighs of annoyance when results are not swift.

Good Things Come to Those Who Wait

As you contemplate the need for change in your life, keep in mind the above adage.

Realize that this time next year you will be different. Your body will have changed, your bank account balance will be altered and your hair color, if you are anything like me, will be from a different box than the one you bought the other day. You will not change in a week, therefore you should be proactive but patient with the process.

Patience Is A Virtue

A virtue involves conforming to a standard of excellence. Just because society moves at a tremendous pace does not mean that you have to operate on the same schedule. When you wait for results, you develop discipline and a better appreciation of the outcome. And most importantly, it guarantees that you won't have to settle for anything less than what you expect. You can work toward your version of perfection without stressing out in the meantime.

So inoculate yourself against the "right now" disease. Take a daily dose of patience, add a dash of faith, mix in a little flexibility and steep it in a large, piping hot cup of humility. Drink this tonic daily while you take a few deep breaths and accept your timetable on your terms.

Relax. Just as my parents have to wait for the rains to replenish their water supply, some things must happen naturally.

Color These Shapes. Stay in the lines. Practice patience.

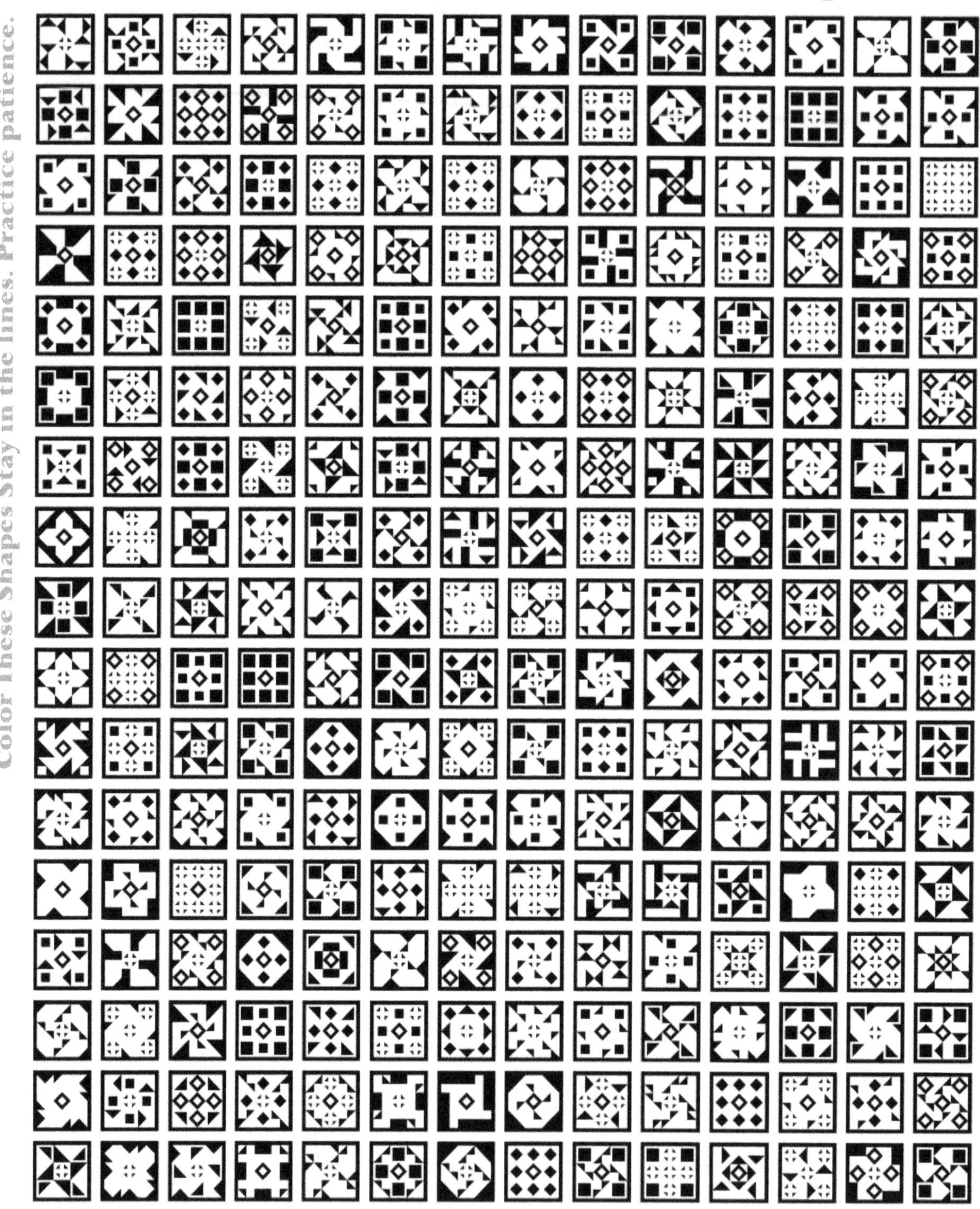

SUNDAY BLOODY SUNDAY

My neighbor Donna brought an interesting thought to my attention recently. We were discussing that we both fight more with our spouses on Sunday. Donna noted that Sunday, the day traditionally set aside for Christians to rest, seek spiritual guidance and rejuvenation is the same day when everything seems to go straight to hell! After a full week of work, errands and responsibilities, we naturally try to keep up the pace on the weekends. Sunday becomes the day to finish projects or get a jumpstart on the week ahead. Yet on the other hand, we simply want to relax, thus becoming annoyed with not being able to. I really think she's on to something here.

Sundays Do Suck

The more I thought about it, my husband and I are more uptight and at odds on Sundays than any other day of the week. We tend to have different expectations about the day. I get the kids ready for church, while he sits at his computer and types. I yell and scream at the kids to get dressed, brush their teeth and wear something decent for God's sake to our local house of worship. He yells and screams about needing some peace and quiet to type up a spreadsheet on his laptop. I break about ten different laws to get us to church on time. He types like a maniac after we leave to get his work done before we come back home. I receive my weekly dose of inspiration, get calm and return home with a new attitude. When I arrive, ready to relax, drink more coffee and read *The Washington Post*, he's done with work and has moved on to the house tasks that are on his "To-Do" list. By the time I'm done reading, he's picked up the dog crap in the yard, cut the grass and weed-wacked around the fence. Now he's ready to do something fun. I have laundry waiting for me and don't really care. He wants to take the kids to the park. I remember the three times already this week that I took the kids to the park while he was at work and don't want to go. He wants to be have "family time." I want some "alone time."

Week Days Versus Weekends

During the week the routine is already set. We know what to expect so we "just do it." But on the weekends our options are more open and we can more readily pick and choose what activities will get our attention. By Sunday we allow our unfinished business to hang over us like a noose making us both anxious and irritable. We try to squeeze in a lot of tasks when we both would rather relax and hangout. And because we don't better honor our need for rest from Monday through Saturday, eventually we lose all gusto and patience with one another.

Visualize Your Perfect Sunday

Take a moment and rethink your Sunday routine. Note if Sundays have this affect on your life as well. For many people it is the last day before the work week recycles itself. For others it's a day to recover from a weekend of excess. Regardless of your religious beliefs Sunday, like Saturday, is designed for family connection.

Unlike the olden days when stores and places of business closed and families gathered for a mid-day meal, now we go to or catch up on work, do home projects, cart our children from a game to a practice to a birthday party and are exhausted by dinnertime.

If you are going to jam pack your weekly schedule anyway, (and you know you will), you owe it to everyone to have one day to re-charge. Whether your day of rest falls on Saturday or Sunday, those two days set the tone for the coming work week so keep that in mind when scheduling your weekend activities. I really think that it's time to reclaim the weekend for reflection, relaxation and renewal. Allow yourself the luxury of customizing a day that nourishes your spirit. Be clear about your expectations and see if it changes the dynamic of your family, eases the stress in your life and improves the well-being of everyone in your home.

Visualize Your Perfect Sunday

Define "rest".

What are the weekend expectations of the members of your family?

Be specific and describe your perfect Sunday.

CONSTANT CHANGE

I remember when my friend, Erzserbet, was preparing to move from Hoboken, New Jersey to the Slovak Republic. I received an email from her in which she stated, "I am getting used to the idea of moving to a country with two children in the middle of the winter while not speaking the language." Now that's a woman who knows how to embrace change!

Change can attack without warning, and you have no choice but to adjust like if you have to move due to a job switch or are diagnosed with a disease that you must fight. Then there are the changes that we consciously choose like going off to college, beginning a new relationship or purposefully conceiving a child.

For a myriad of reasons, we have all been faced with change and survived. Some handle it with poise and dignity. Others fight it tooth and nail, wasting a lot of energy in the process. Regardless, leaving your comfort zone, even an uncomfortable comfort zone, can create apprehension and fear. Knowing what to expect, even when it is awful, is sometimes much easier than facing what is unknown and mysterious. Since change is inevitable, here are some tips to help you navigate change with ease:

You Are Fully Equipped to Handle Change. Take a moment and honor the fact that you have looked change straight in the eye and won. You have changed jobs, hairdos, addresses, major appliances and maybe even spouses. You have everything that you need to create change in your life. Chances are whatever accomplishments you feel are no big deal impress the heck out of somebody. Someone out there is in awe of you whether or not you understand how fabulous you are.

Positive Feedback Strengthens People to Move Forward. If you want to create positive change in your own life, always, take a moment to tell someone else that they are doing a good job. When you see your friend and she looks great, don't just think it - tell her! When a first-time mom walks into a room with a newborn strapped to her chest, no makeup on, greasy hair and dark circles under her eyes, remind her what an amazing job she is doing. When the new gal at works makes 18 mistakes before lunch, remember your first day on the job and mention the 20 mistakes you made. Positive thoughts and remarks have an energy that once sent out into the world, gain momentum and come back to you. By encouraging others, you ultimately create encouragement that will return to you threefold.

You must do the work required to create change.

Graciously Accept the Positive Energy That You Receive. When someone compliments or encourages you, thank them! Don't give them ten reasons why they are wrong. Accept the comment and allow it to propel you forward.

Associate With People That Lift You Up. Sometimes we erroneously believe that if we hang around with people that are down and out like ourselves and expend our energy complaining, they will better understand us and therefore help us in some way. However, negative energy returns to you as well. The more negativity you create, the more you will eventually have to deal with.

Accept That Change Requires Work. I used to watch guests on Oprah state how a certain sentence in a certain book changed their life. So of course, I would run out and buy that book. I'd be on the last page wondering where the hell that sentence was that was going to miraculously change my life for me. Then I realized that...

Change Requires Action. Having an "Oprah Show Light Bulb Moment" works like the flick of a switch. Yes it is instantaneous, but you still have to pay your electric

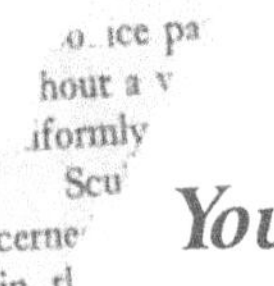

You have infinite possibilities. . .

bill, change the bulb and dust the outer lampshade every once in a while to keep the light burning bright. You must do the work required to create change.

Change Involves Having a Plan – Or Not! Now this one is tricky. Planning takes time and can become the thing that you do instead of actually changing. The newsletter I used to write is a great example. If had planned it out in advance no one would have received their monthly copy. Instead I would get an idea, begin to write only to almost magically come across a cool quote or an interesting article until voila, it got done. It was more time efficient to write while I planned instead of planning to write.

Expect Failure Along the Way
So let's recap. Start with an idea. Take action and embrace the work (even if it's hard), while associating with people that make you feel good. Accept their positive feedback and constantly give it in return. Sounds easy enough. So what's the problem? Why do we attempt yet fail to create change?

I believe it has a lot to do with a lack of self-acceptance. We believe that happiness is dependent upon successful change. But when we start from a place of disrespect for ourselves, the missteps that are bound to occur only increase our level of self or situational loathing. Lessons that we need to learn become characterized as failures. Normal developments in the process become blocks or obstacles. We have so much riding on the goals we set that we become rigid with outcomes, narrowing our windows of opportunity.

Small Changes Count
Change is the act of modifying and making different or replacing something all together. Many women focus on their ultimate outcome instead of recognizing when they've taken the necessary small steps needed to achieve their goal. Thus when their actions result in a change in the details, they don't give themselves enough credit. A looser pair of jeans is a success even if the numbers on the scale haven't budged. If someone compliments you on the new coat of paint don't respond, "Well, I still need to buy a couch and hang some pictures." Allow yourself to be happy with where you are in the process.

Set Your Limits
Change is a verb. It is what you do to become content. But being, as in being content, is also a verb. It involves limiting yourself in requirements, actions and desires. So if you are going to consciously attempt to create change, to be successful you must also consciously attempt to limit what you need to be happy as well. There is no doubt in my mind that you can have it all. But if you don't define what "all" is, you are going to drive yourself crazy. The all that we give as well as receive is different for each one of us. Limiting yourself firmly grounds you in reality, allowing you to notice the smaller successes in your life. This focus allows you to embrace your accomplishments and do the above steps with dignity and grace. This allows the bigger picture, your "all" to flourish.

Allow yourself to be happy with where you are in the process.

Reaching a goal is like painting a picture. You have infinite possibilities that are limited by the size of the canvas. After a few brush strokes you must step back and view the proportions to know where to add color, texture, shadow and light, then return your focus back to the details. It's the balance of these two things that create the art. Just as it is the balance between action and acceptance that creates positive and lasting change.

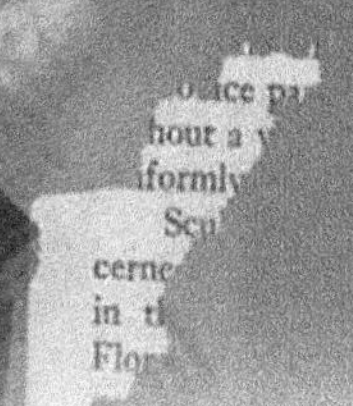

List a few major changes that have occurred in your life in the past :

- ***Decade:***

- ***Year:***

- ***Month:***

- ***Week:***

Which changes were difficult to adjust to? Which changes were easy to implement?

Think about changes that were forced upon you versus those that you chose for yourself.

Set a timer and write for 5 minutes while reflecting on the word, CHANGE.

Don't Think – Just Write . . . GO!

I change masks frequently

Put On Your Mask

I loved dressing up for Halloween as a child, even though I was forced to wear cheap plastic masks with off centered eye-holes, plugged up nose-holes and sharp mouth edges that cut like a razor through the flesh on my lips. By the third house on the trick or treat route, the rubber-band that kept the mask attached to my head would break, so Mom would reattach it with another knot. This process continued until the mask became too tight to wear and was transformed into a sun visor on top of my head.

Being from the north, I wore a winter coat over my costume. This added to the confusion and required me to explain to each treat giver that I really was the Bionic Woman underneath my parka. By then the mystery was gone and I focused on finding the homeowners handing out full-sized candy bars while avoiding the killjoys handing out toothpaste samples or raisins.

No matter how cool my costume was, it always disappointed me when I had to give in and remove my mask. I enjoyed pretending to be 1970 heroines such as Wonder Woman and Almighty Isis. Pretending to be someone I wasn't in order to get treats was a challenge, whereas being myself and schlepping for candy felt like charity.

Masks Are Good

Masks are not only fun and interesting, but also necessary. From a functional perspective a hockey goalie would not play without a mask and if a surgeon entered my sterile field without her mask, I'd be out of there faster than you can say, "malpractice lawsuit."

In ancient Greece, masks worn by performers allowed actors to play various roles while enabling the Grecians in the cheap seats to see the expressions that were being conveyed on the stage. The mask doubled as a megaphone, allowing patrons to hear the dialogue as

well. It was the mask that enabled concepts to be communicated and commentaries to be made.

By All Means, Keep Your Mask On

I appreciate when someone wears her "everything is okay" mask if I bump into her in the grocery store. Chances are that I'm in a hurry. The last thing I want is to be trapped in the cold aisle listening to someone complain ad nauseam about her life.

I change masks frequently along with the personas that accompany them. I never wear my "I'm so sexy" mask when caring for my children because that would just be wrong and could lead to years of therapy for them. Similarly, I try to remove my "the kids are driving me to drink" mask when connecting intimately with my husband. And if you're a guy giving me the creeps, I'll don my "touch me and I will kill you" mask in a heartbeat.

Masks Are Necessary

Self-help gurus encourage people to "take off their masks." I understand that this is a metaphor used to encourage people to live authentically. But this approach to personal growth, I believe, gives the misguided impression that there is only one you that you present to the world when actually there are many sides to your personality that you reveal based on the time, place and situation.

Your assertive mask keeps you on track. Your aggressive mask keeps you safe. Your vulnerable mask tells the world that you could use some help and are open to receiving it and your fun-and-frolic mask keeps your appointment calendar filled with interesting things to do. Don't confuse the functional daily uses of your various masks with being inauthentic. You are simply being practical and appropriate, and don't allow anyone tell you otherwise.

Embrace Your Various Masks

Instead of discarding all of your masks, reflect on how each one assists you. Examine them and make any necessary adjustments. Cut out larger holes around the eyes so that you can see the entire world and not just two feet in front of you. Make sure that you can breathe while wearing it instead of sucking it up against your face with every inhalation. Enlarge the mouth area so that your words can escape your lips and reach the people that you need to communicate with. And by all means, replace the darn rubber band so that it fits comfortably on your head. You'll know which masks to keep because the necessary ones will mold to you like a second skin. It's only the fake ones that flip up like visors making you look like a dork, so feel free to throw those out.

Sometimes the people you need to connect with are far away, up in the bleachers getting a nosebleed. Your mask may be exactly what they require to enjoy the show and gain the wisdom that they have been searching for. And it may be just the mask that you need to wear to have the courage to authentically express yourself to them as well.

Instead of discarding all of your masks, reflect on how each one assists you.

Label this mask. Write the names of all the different masks that you wear.

Your Mission If You Choose to Accept It

"There are always two points of view about yourself – yours, and the opinion of people who love you. Our opinion is that we're a mess, a fraud, maybe vaguely disgusting. But others seem to love us, to feel great relief that we are in their lives. So one of these opinions is wrong, and you get to choose which one to believe." ~ Anne Lamott

Be Grateful

The next time you receive a Valentine's Day , birthday, mother's day, anniversary or "just thinking of you" card, be grateful. Say thank-you. Maybe even gush a little about how thoughtful this person was to send a token of their appreciation on 10% post consumer recycled paper. Just don't say, "Ah, you shouldn't have."

Look

When you gingerly open it (rather than shaking it to see if any money falls out), take in the colors, shapes, images and textures. Notice the care and creativity used to create the card and think about the time that person spent selecting it just for you.

Read

Perhaps you'll quickly scan the card, focusing less on the text and wondering more about whether a dozen roses or a piece of jewelry will soon be presented to you. Don't do that.

Focus on the words. The card will probably mention something about how wonderful you are. How your love is all that matters. How your presence in this person's life makes all the difference.

Listen

Will you believe the card? When you read it will you feel validated or like a vaguely disgusting fraud? Will you understand your importance in the life of the sender? Will you understand that it is specifically your connection to this person that allows him or her to thrive?

Believe

If you do not recognize the words as an accurate description of yourself, then read them again. Really drink in the message and swish it about. Enjoy the tastes and textures while savoring each flavorful word. Allow the sentiments to fuel you by making the choice to believe this person's opinion of you. Be brave enough to see yourself through the eyes of someone that loves you.

Decide

Then choose to adapt this opinion as your own.

If you know that you are scared, you can fight it, but if you don't know you're scared, it can be really crippling. I opted unconsciously to avoid ever finding out if I was good enough by not following through. ~ *Lucy Kaplansky*

Follow through . . .

Notes

What story from this book resonated with you?

Random Reactions

WHAT PART OF THIS BOOK DID YOU THINK WAS COMPLETE AND UTTER B.S.?

If you had an Oprah show "A-Ha Moment" while reading this book, deconstruct it here:

KEEN OBSERVATIONS

Write your own self-help junkie story here:

Express Yourself

Collage Page #1:

Let this book inspire you to create your own collages.

COLLAGE PAGE #2

www.ingramcontent.com/pod-product-compliance
Ingram Content Group UK Ltd.
Pitfield, Milton Keynes, MK11 3LW, UK
UKHW051129260726
13967UKWH00010B/2938